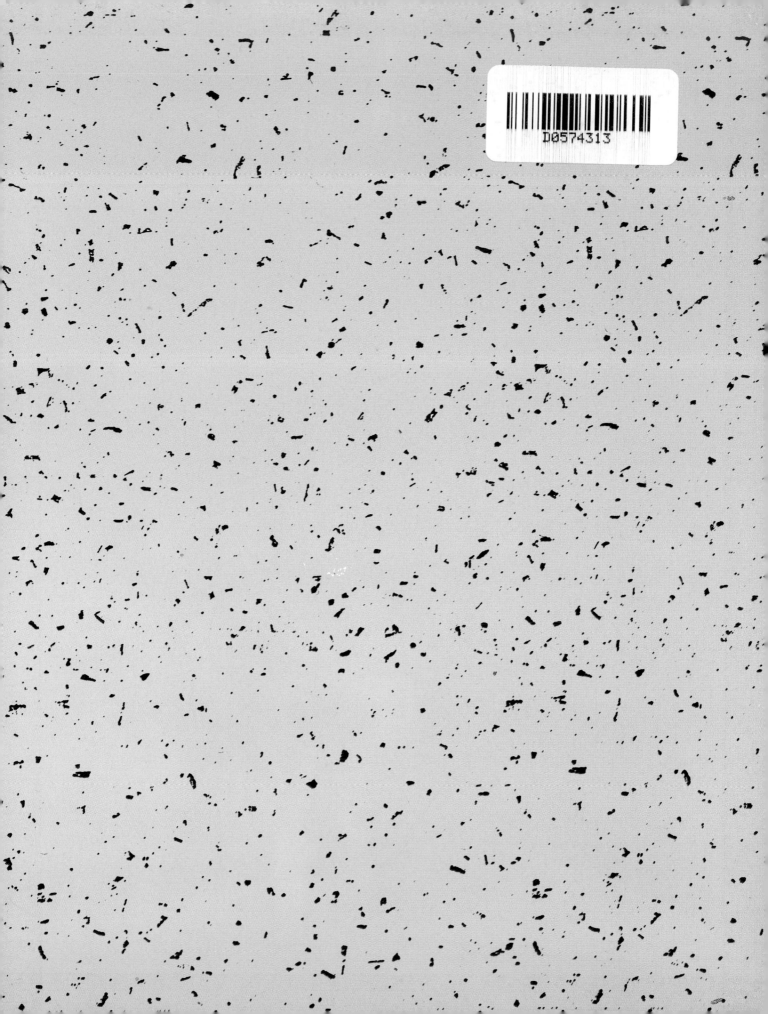

BETH ELON

THE BIG BOOK OF PASTA

September 12, 2002

For dear Frieda,

on the occasion of your birthday —
a gift for a cook who makes
meatballs with matzoh meal.

with love.

27

BETH ELON

THE BIG BOOK OF PASTA

Photographs: Nelly Sheffer
Illustrations: Hili Hillman

Kosher

MODAN PUBLISHING HOUSE

THE BIG BOOK OF PASTA
by
Beth Elon

Book Design: Studio Ruth Rahat

Food Styling: Bella Rudnik

Typesetting: Modan Publishing House
Montage: Y.S. Offset

Photographic props were loaned by Casa Viva. Tel-Aviv; Blue Bandana. Herzlia
Pituah; Danish Plus, Tel-Aviv; Pastalina, Tel-Aviv; Sycamore, Tel-Aviv; Galeria
Darwish, Tel-Aviv; and Kad al Hayam, Tel-Aviv.

Special thanks to Bella and Elkana Levy, Kafria, Rishpon; to Monique Ben-Zaken,
of Mamma Mia Restaurant, Jerusalem; to Tamar Segri.

Printed in Israel, 1996

CONTENTS

TO AMOS AND DANAE

With grateful acknowledgement

As with many other books, and cookbooks in particular, this book could never have been written without the help and kindness of friends and colleagues. I would like to thank my Italian friends and neighbors, who not only kindly agreed to taste unusual, and to them rather odd, pastas, but also warmly encouraged me - the stranger living among them - to never feel like an intruder.

Thanks to Hili Hillman, who applied her special talents to the drawings in this book, and to Nelly Sheffer, whose love for pasta is well reflected in his photographs. Also, to Bella Rudnik for her superb taste and inventiveness in bringing variety to the photo backgrounds. And to Amos Elon for his constant devoted participation in eating and editing.

DISCOVERING

PASTA

CHAPTER ONE

This book is the result of many years spent partly in Italy, on a small farm in the soft rolling hills of Tuscany, where the delights of Italian cooking became a sensuous discovery. I learned there how wonderfully varied a well-prepared plate of pasta can be, that the combination of sauces made from fresh vegetables, dairy products, meat or fish can be virtually endless. It was there that pasta became a regular staple of our daily diet, tasty and nourishing, and best of all, as it turned out, not even fattening.

Pasta as a course in almost every meal is one of the deeply rooted traditions so integral a part of Italian rural life. Even today, as Italians - like all of us - eat less, the pasta shelves that take up the largest single space in the supermarket are wiped clean each week. The most profound impression one comes away with after spending time in a small Italian village is the sense of permanence and tradition that pervades in a landscape that sways, unbroken, with all currents, be they natural, cultural, or even political.

Drought and flooding strike Tuscany with amazing regularity. Frost and withering heat, winds and storms, continually ravage the rugged terraced hills destroying vegetation and eroding carefully controlled crops. Yet nothing deters the Tuscan farmer from pursuing his annual cycle of planting and reaping the same crops, in the same months, on the same side of the moon (waning), as he has done for centuries. True, farmers are leaving the soil to make an easier living. But it is rare to find a home without its own *orto*, a kitchen garden, from which to pluck the daily lot of vegetables for the table. Food is abundant and fresh, in spite of an ever present lament. During every season vegetables fresh from the garden abound on the table.

Along with this deeply rooted sense of permanence comes a tradition of preparation and eating of food that has taken on the sensuality of the surrounding soft landscape of terraced olive groves and vineyards. Dining is a way of life. Twice a day the family sits together to a meal in which every course is a pleasure to look at and a delight to the palate. Nothing is served simply to fill the empty stomach; each dish must serve the senses as well. The result of centuries of such dining is a rich blend of tastes, that today is as much a part of the Tuscan soul as is the way of village life.

The Tuscan insists very much on doing things his own way. I learned this quite abruptly early on when I offered a bowl of Israeli *hoummus* as my contribution to a village festival. *Ceci* (chick peas) served with lemon, parsley and olive oil is a well loved and oft-served dish in the village; a plate of the same, only mashed as *hoummus*, was unacceptable. Polite as they were, the only reaction I heard was a reserved *"hmm, molto interessante, signora, come si fa?"* ("Hmm, very interesting signora, how do you make it?").

Our friend and neighbor, Signor Biondi, is well into his eighties, but still spends his entire day on a formerly abandoned parcel of land nearby that he has turned into a pleasing vista of terraced vegetables, grape vines and full olive trees. And he still has time and patience to lend a sympathetic ear and hand to my superficial but wholehearted farming enthusiasm. He often comes up to our house - usually bearing a sack of fresh eggs or a bottle of this year's wine - along with his *zappa*, a sturdy hoe which seems to serve for almost every local farming chore, ostensibly to show me the correct way to hoe, or to seed, or to weed, or to fertilize, or even just to *zap*. But, as he shows and explains, Mr. Biondi always manages to finish the chore himself, with amazing ease and grace, in a matter of minutes, as I chase after him calling, *"Si, si, Signor Biondi, gia capisco, adesso faccio io!"* (Okay, okay, Signor Biondi, I understand, now let me do it.") But there it is, all beautifully done, lines of tomatoes, or beans, tied together in an intricate tent scaffolding of freshly-hewn reed poles both practical and aesthetic, or vines cut properly back to their third knot and tied against their frames, or sulphur scattered in just the exact amounts into the beautifully "zapped" furrows between rows of vegetables.

Other neighbors continually teach me delightful new ways to use our fresh and abundant vegetables. (I have my own ways as well, but as patiently as they listen, my neighbors are rarely open to an untried suggestion.) Our beloved friend, italicize penne, in her sixties with the strength and fortitude to transform a rocky field of overgrown grass into a rich bed of potatoes, garlic, spring onions and bushes of artichoke, using only the simple *zappa* as a tool, often invites us to come and share the family meal. These days, her daughter-in-law, Giuliana, has joined her in both making the *orto* and preparing the meal. Giusseppina's favorite pasta is a mix of short *penne*, fresh broccoli, garlic and oil, all cooked together in a beautiful pastiche and serve up with slabs of fresh country bread to dip into the leftover garlicky oil sauce. The recipe is in Chapter 9.

Anita, who occasionally passes by to say "hello", lends her advice on pruning back the red and white currant bushes she gave us several years ago. Her special invitation is to a lasagna supper, which is of the sort no Tuscan would dream of. Anita is originally from Benevento, in the south, where a lasagna means a substantial dish of pasta layers interspersed with slices of sausage, hard-boiled eggs, chopped meat, various vegetables and just about anything else that happens to be lying about the larder, all smothered in a rich tomato and cheese sauce. (The Tuscan lasagna - at least in our parts - is made of little more than tomato sauce, Parmesan and mozzarella spread between the thinnest fresh pasta slabs. Heavenly.)

Angelina, who many years ago taught me the patient art of kneading dough, is gone now, but the beautiful blue *hortense* she brought us still bloom and multiply each year. Gone, too, is Lorenzo, but the hazelnuts he planted for us still provide warm annual memories of his friendship and love of the soil. And each time we sit to a simple pasta of fresh oil, garlic and anchovies, I think of Lorenzo's simple hardworking way of life, and how very filled with creativity and productivity it was.

For years, it was Emilio's wife Giovanna, who often came to us laden with fresh eggs and freshly made *schiacciata* - the salty flat bread that once seemed so particular to our village, and is now so popular everywhere. *"Per la bimba"*, she would announce, for our daughter who grew up partly as a little Tuscan. Giovanna still brings us her freshly made delights, even though the bimba is now a young woman. The jams we exchange with so many of the village women each summer find their way back to our home in Israel, where we can delight in Tuscan memories the entire year.

The meals we share with our Italian friends and their families are among the most pleasurable one can imagine. I once thought that theirs was not really a sophisticated, or fine, cuisine. Today, Italian rustic food is sought after and appreciated throughout our world. The centuries-old care and culinary art that goes into each course is these days imitated by the finest restaurants. Finding fresh olive oil, fruity and rich from the first pressing, has become a major challenge for the best restaurant chefs; young wines, simple and unsophisticated with no additives, are served with pleasure and pride; vegetables and fruits plucked from the garden in the morning to serve with a freshly-slaughtered chicken are the boast of the most desirable dining places.

Dining is a major part of our Italian pleasure, mostly, I think, because of the close sensual ties the food shares with its surroundings. But we are still newcomers to the experience, and as such have been able to develop our own pace and methods in the preparation and serving of the local fare. Early on we discovered that a typical Italian meal of antipasto, minestra (either soup or pasta), meat and all the trimmings was simply too much for us at a single sitting, and it became our habit to eliminate courses and add only a salad, fruit and cheese accompaniment. (Recently many Italian families have as well, given the new emphasis on lighter eating everywhere.)

Our entertaining follows the same pattern, and it is an easy invitation to ask both Italian and and foreign friends to come over to share a pasta. Convivial, simple and relaxing, it has become our way of entertaining close friends and neighbors informally and inexpensively, and creatively as well. As foreigners, we are allowed to be a bit mad, a bit different, and as a result, each new pasta I come up with is indulged with affection, and sometimes even enthusiasm.

It is just as easy to entertain in the same fashion at home. We are not very big sweet eaters, and I confess to a certain boredom with baking cakes. As a consequence, while I love to spend hours of relaxed fussing in the kitchen, a talent for baking and sweet-making still eludes. Entertaining friends after dinner for an evening of drinks, coffee and cakes is simply a chore. The great fun is to entertain friends in an informal manner, at an early hour, when they can arrive fresh and hungry, and leave at a decent time as well. Especially during the work week.

The pleasure of entertaining in this way has afforded me the challenge of creating new ways to serve pasta, seeking to adapt without expecting the exact tastes one can find only in Italy. The recipes in this book are the result of probing, experimenting and developing, and I would encourage the reader to do the same.

My own Number One rule is: Don't be a purist. Pasta as we know it is certainly an Italian invention - originally brought back, 'tis said, by Marco Polo, from a trip to the Orient. There is, however, evidence that it was eaten in the eastern Mediterranean even before the Roman conquest. Today everybody looks for fresh ideas with pasta. Even Italians are experimenting with new pastas, both warm and cold, and come up with combinations that a few years ago would have been anathema to any self-respecting Italian.

Pasta has certainly achieved its culinary heights in Italian cuisine, but Italian cuisine has a heady Mediterranean aura which we can share as well. The world has synthesized itself into a single supermarket, and there is little that is not available to all. But substitutions can often be practical; if an item for a particular recipe is not at hand, try another. Your family will appreciate the variety that is so simple to bring into the family diet. So will your friends.

Inexpensive, nutritious, and even not fattening. It was a marvel to discover that Italians who eat pasta twice a day are as slim as our weight-watching compatriots, who gasp at the very thought of a plate of spaghetti (yet easily manage to put away any number of rich creamy desserts). Pasta can certainly be overindulged, like everything else worth eating. As normal fare, however, once or even twice a week, it is no more fattening than a dish of meat and potatoes. We as a family, over the years, have been enjoying a pasta (or rice) dish almost daily. We may not be skinny, but none of us has really gained unnecessary weight.

ON BUYING
PASTA

CHAPTER TWO

As we've noted, there has been a virtual pasta revolution over the past few years, a revolution that has done only good.

Durum wheat is now used for every dried variety of pasta, and the varieties are endless. Perhaps not the hundreds of different shapes one finds in Italy, but enough variety to keep most consumers happy.

A word about durum wheat. The use of durum wheat in a dried pasta makes the difference between a pasta that holds its shape and one that sogs lifelessly when cooked. Durum wheat is a special, hard-grained, high protein wheat that, in a process of prolonged, gradual drying, assures a firm bite, resiliency and long life. (Durum is Latin for "hard".)

Durum wheat contains more protein than either potatoes or rice, and has a less starchy, less "floury" taste than noodles using any other kind of flour. This is noticeable even in the cooking water; when the durum wheat pasta has finished cooking, the water will not be cloudy with starch. When drained, the pasta will not stick together in the colander. It need never be rinsed after cooking, nor should it ever be.

If one sticks to Italian names, the vast variety of pastas can become a tongue-twisting exercise in memory retention. They roll off the tongue in a melodious aria: the familiar spaghetti, surrounded by *spaghettini* and *fedelini* (both slim spaghettis), *tortelloni* and *tortellini* (large and little stuffed pastas), *linguini* (tongue-shaped), *orecchiette* (ears), *tagliatelle* and *fettuccine* (long flat noodles), *quadrucci* (little squares), *penne* and *rigatoni* (short tubed shapes, one ridged, the other smooth), *ziti* (a narrower rigatoni), *ruote di carro* (spiked wheel shapes), *bucatini* and *perciatelli* (both hollow, thick, long noodles), *chitarrini, ditali, conchiglie* and *conchiglini* (big and little shells), *farfalle* and *strichetti* (butterfly or bowtie shapes), *fusilli* or *eliche* (screwlike short pastas), *maccheroni* and *maccheroncini*. Those are but a few. The list goes on and on, confused even further by the fact that the same pasta can be called differently from one Italian region to another. The result, at least for the smitten foreigner, is a mass of confusion to be succumbed to with the same spirited indulgence with which one succumbs to Italian opera. (My favorite pasta name is one called *strangolaprete,* which means it can strangle a priest.)

Following is a glossary of almost all the pasta shapes one finds in durum wheat pastas.

As you develop your own pasta sense, you'll know which pastas go best with which sauces. (Some sauces just want to cling to a thin *spaghettini;* others want to fill in and around a *penne,* or *conchiglie.* Most go well with any pasta you have on hand.)

THE LONG PASTAS:

Spaghetti: The noodle we all know and love, and the name often wrongly applied to all pastas. It goes well with just about any sauce.

Spaghettini and Fedelini: Thinner, more delicate versions of spaghetti that call for somewhat lighter sauces. Both go well with the simplest of condiments, olive oil and garlic, or butter and cheese. Best for smooth sauces.

Linguini: Long, flat, almost ovally shaped in its thickness. If available I choose it over all the others. *Linguini* has a slightly slick surface, which some may find less preferable, but it definitely holds a sauce better than any others.

Tagliatelle and Fettuccine: The long, wide, flat noodles that seem to be made for a butter and cheese sauce, or for the classic *ragu* of Bologna. *Fettuccine* is almost always a fresh egg pasta; *tagliatelle* is sold both fresh and dried. *Tagliatelle* is more a northern name; *fettuccine* is Roman. Both are the easiest noodles to make at home, given their wide flat shape.

Maccheroni: The tubular version of spaghetti, that comes either long or short. Children love it, and a similar version with an even larger hole - called *Bucatini* - as well.

Lasagne: The wide, flat pasta that is used almost exclusively as a layer in oven casseroles of the same name, and originally made with a combination of two sauces: *ragu* and bechamel. *Lasagne* can be made with dried or fresh pasta; the dry version usually needs precooking before assembling the lasagne. The fresh does not require it, if the sauce is liquid enough. Today *lasagne* can be made with almost any sauce combined with bechamel.

THE SHORTER PASTAS:

Penne: Probably the most popular of the shorter pastas. In its most basic version it is a short, smooth tubular pasta cut diagonally at both ends. Penne Rigate are the same, but have a ridged rather than smooth surface. Either one goes wonderfully with any sauce that has chunks of anything in it, vegetables or meat. Less sauce goes further with them as well.

Rigatoni: Also short and tubular, they are thicker than *penne,* ridged along the sides and cut off flat at both ends. Good for the same sauces that go well with *penne.*

Maccheroncini: Short, fat and tubular, rounded and smooth. Similar to the *chimeric* and *macaroncelli.* They all can be found ridged as well, and are wonderful in oven casseroles that call for melted cheese; they hold their firmness well when baked again in their sauce. Also good for buffet dishes. Generally speaking, the short pastas are easily eaten in forkfuls while standing.

Farfalle (Butterflies) or Strichetti (bow ties): An interchangeable name, in any event one almost indistinguishable from the other. (The *farfalle* have pointed corners, the *strichetti* rounded.) Both can be found in two sizes. A fairly light sauce is recommended for the larger; the smaller can be used in thick soups and light casseroles.

Fusilli, Eliche, or Spirali: The corkscrew pastas, another favorite of the young. They are particularly good with meat and vegetable *ragus* where pieces of meat or vegetables can gather in their folds. For a quick children's supper, however, they are wonderful with just a coating of butter and cheese. Good in cold salads too.

Conchiglie and conchiglini: Big shells and little shells, both very popular. Use the big ones in sauces that have bits of meat or vegetables; they can also be cooked, stuffed and baked in the oven... an effort I don't find particularly rewarding. The little *conchiglini* are nicest with a lighter sauce and no bits and

A most important element in any well-prepared pasta dish is the proper cooking of the pasta itself. A mushy pasta bathed in caviar will still taste like mushy pasta. Thus the Italian expression, al dente, *has entered the language of international cuisine, and has become as familiar as terms like* largo *or* allegro *in the world of music.*

Al dente *means, literally, to the bite, and denotes, in culinary language, that the pasta - or rice or whatever - is cooked thoroughly, firm to the bite, but not a whit mushy. Unless it is an oven dish, pasta should never be prepared beforehand. Sauce can be waiting, water can be salted and boiling, but the pasta goes in only when it's ready to be served. An Italian housewife will drop the pasta into the already boiling water as she hears the last diner arriving.*

I can remember Italian dinner hostesses telephoning as we were about to leave for their dinner parties to ask if we would be on time; the pasta was about to be put to boil and heaven help us all if it should have to wait. A bit of an exaggeration; the more normal proceeding is to hold off until the guests have all arrived before dropping the pasta in. (The well-salted water simmers as we wait.)

EQUIPMENT

Very little in the way of special equipment is required to properly boil pasta. There are splendid pots available these days, something like couscous makers, with a colander that holds any length of pasta and fits right into a larger pan to be filled with water. The colander filled with the perfect *al dente* pasta then just gets pulled out . When buying such a pan, however, remember that pasta requires a large amount of water in which to cook well. A pan bought with pasta in mind should be ready to hold well over 20 cups of water in addition to the pasta. A light pan that boils water quickly is perfectly adequate for the task. Be sure to wash it thoroughly after each use; light pots have a way of collecting calcium deposits that, if not thoroughly washed out, can have an effect on future pasta tastes.

A long-handled wooden fork or spatula, to help separate strands and keep the pasta from sticking to the bottom of the pan, is also handy. Again, new devices are available for just that purpose; the best looking and most practical is undoubtedly the wooden one with nine pegs sticking out from the rounded top. It works well separating both thin strands and short fat pastas. (The pasta should be separated as soon as it gets into the water.) There are also less attractive plastic devices that serve well.

For *gnocchi,* stuffed pastas and lasagne noodles, you'll want a slotted spoon, or, better yet, a slotted spatula, to gently remove the individual pieces as they finish cooking without either breaking up the pastas or disturbing the remaining boiling pastas.

The final absolute necessity is a large colander, preferably one with side handles that can rest on the side of a bowl or basin.

Oven-baked pastas require various-sized baking dishes that will fill to the brim and are attractive to the eye. It's a matter of taste, but earthenware, or large, plain white oven dishes seem the most natural for a hearty and colorful pasta meal.

THE COOKING

There are two inviolate rules in the cooking of pasta: use plenty of water, and plenty of salt. Together they will enhance the taste of your pasta and prevent it from turning out starchy or gluey. Durum wheat never clouds the water and should NEVER be rinsed.

Plan 4 cups of water for each $3^1/_2$ ounces of pasta. The amount of pasta needed for each diner depends very much on what else is being served, and how light or heavy a meal is planned. The rule in Italy - where pasta serves only as a first course - used to be 100 grams, or $3^1/_2$ ounces per serving. With an increasingly diet-conscious population, the rule today is more like one pound of pasta as a first course for five or six people. For a main course, 4 ounces per diner is a good rule of thumb. It's always better to have some leftover than not enough, and one can always use leftover pasta - chopped and mixed with some eggs - fried up into a *frittata*. Even just heated in the microwave and served afresh is not out of the question.

Most of the recipes in this book are for a 1 or 1.1 pound package of pasta. But sauces can be stretched to cover a larger amount; if the final dish seems too dry, or too sparse, add a little more oil, butter, tomato concentrate, or whatever liquid is being used as the base for the sauce. Often a tablespoon or two of the water in which the pasta has been cooked will make the sauce more liquid, and stretch it to cover a larger amount of pasta.

To each 4 cups of pasta cooking water, add a heaping teaspoon of coarse cooking salt. Best time to add is just after the water has come to its first boil. Add the salt and allow the water to boil again. It is not really necessary to add oil to the pan when there is plenty of water, although some cooks do. If the pan does not hold all the water necessary for the amount of pasta, then by all means add the oil; it may keep the strands from sticking. (This is one of those fine points of pasta cookery where there seems to be no general agreement; of such points there are many.)

When the water returns to a rapid, rolling boil after the salt has been added (this is best accomplished with the lid on), add the pasta, all at once. Open all the packages at one end beforehand, and slide the pasta over the edge of the pan into the water. With short pastas, just dump it in all at once. Now is the time for the pronged pasta mixer. As soon as all the pasta is in the water, mix it well and make sure nothing is sticking, either to itself or to the bottom of the pan. Put on the lid, bring quickly back to the boil, uncover and mix again, separating all the strands. When the pasta is soft enough to carry on by itself, let it cook.

Check the cooking time on the pasta package, but don't take it too seriously. When the pasta has lost its shine, and begins to look edible, draw out a strand, or a noodle, and bite into it. If it is still tough, throw it back and try again a minute later. (A certified pasta chef once told me that a pasta was done the minute it stuck to the wall. It was his habit to draw out a strand, pitch it against the nearest wall, and test. If it stayed put, it was cooked. I don't know what he did with those that didn't stick, but the bite test seems just as reliable.)

The instant you can bite through the pasta with no resistance, it is done. Remove it immediately from the flame, and throw in a small glassful of cold water to stop the cooking. Drain it right away and mix the sauce in immediately. Your diners should be waiting.

YOUR PASTA
CUPBOARD

CHAPTER FOUR

Freshly-made egg pasta has become part of our lives. Fresh pasta shops provide all shapes and types of pasta - thin *spaghetti* and thick *fettuccine*, flat *lasagne* and filled *ravioli* and *tortellini*. Reach into any supermarket freezer, and come up with any number of little sacks of green, red/orange or just plain yellow pastas. Some are better than others; most can easily be bettered by doing it yourself.

The availability of freshly-made pasta can, I hope, entice the adventurous into making their own at home. The vast choice of diverse fillings to make oneself - from the ordinary ricotta/spinach to smoked salmon and even caviar - can hopefully lead us into the temptation to try new ones of our own. The pasta you make at home will often turn out more delicate, thinner and smoother than anything you'll find in a shop. This is true especially in the case of the filled pastas; the store-bought machine-made varieties rarely melt in the mouth the way those made freshly by hand do. The flour you use at home is the softest, supplest all-purpose; those bought fresh in a shop must often necessarily be made with a flour that will last a while on the shelf and not dry into a brittle pile of crumbs. The durum wheat that makes the best dry pasta makes the best store-bought fresh egg pasta as well.

Freshly made pasta does not necessarily mean better pasta. It is simply different, and the difference is not always a qualitative one. Unlike the ordinary dried durum wheat pasta, which is made without eggs and can serve some sauces much more favorably, the richer fresh pasta contains a number of eggs in its dough. Freshly-made pasta takes less cooking. Made at home, it is still moist when dropped into the pot, and takes only a few minutes to pop to the surface of the boiling water, ready to serve. And, because of the richer quality, less goes further. It often needs less dressing to make the pasta appealing.

A relaxed lazy morning spent rolling and stuffing little thin tartlets with succulent fillings, or layering a lasagne with freshly rolled-out squares, will reap its praise and rewards at the table.

Freshly-made pasta should never be over-stuffed or smothered in sauce. *Ravioli* are not *kreplach,* or *wonton. Cannelloni* are not blintzes. *Ravioli, cannelloni* or *tortellini*, or any other stuffed pasta should be light, the dough rolled out to its thinnest, the stuffing no more than a complement, and the sauce on top just sufficient. Simple butter and grated cheese is perfect for vegetable-filled stuffed pastas; or an olive oil steeped with fresh herbs and salt. A light tomato sauce goes beautifully atop a meat-filled tartlet. And remember to maintain a light touch with the sauce as well; stuffed pastas should never be drowned.

The coloring of pasta is mostly an aesthetic pleasure. Today one sees red/orange - and sometimes other colors - along with the more traditional green. Green means made with spinach, and red/orange pasta is made with the juice of a tomato. Never are vegetable colorings used; the cooked vegetable, water removed, is worked into the dough. Today, even in Italy, impressively packaged pastas made with all sorts of tasty additions tempt the eye: garlic, herb, dried porcini or hot chili peppers. I find them not only expensive, but self-defeating as well; the taste is not particularly distinctive and the pastas become rather heavy and sticky in the process of imbuing all those flavors. Better to use fresh vegetables and fresh tastes in the sauce, and keep the pasta

light and accommodating.

Homemade pastas - including the stuffed ones - can be frozen for a week or two without suffering. Slightly dried to keep them from sticking, dusted with smallest grained semolina (durum wheat) and arranged in layers separated by waxed paper, they should then be tightly wrapped in aluminum foil and frozen. When ready to use, just take them out and toss the frozen pasta into a pan of boiling salted water.

There was a time when freshly-made pasta - just like freshly-made bread - was a daily or weekly event. Today, most of us consider both bread and pasta making too time-consuming. We've lost something; pasta making can provide a rewarding, even relaxing few hours in the kitchen. And good fresh pasta is a lot easier to make than good fresh bread. Filled pasta especially can be an original creative way to bring something totally new to the table. With the aid of a small, handcranked pasta machine, it is not even hard work. (Although many friends use them, I can't recommend those sophisticated all-in-one pasta makers; just the cleaning is a forbidding process.)

ON BEGINNING

It takes some practice to turn out the perfect pasta dough. With time and experience, we can begin to sense the right elasticity when the dough is ready, and even the correct amounts of ingredients, which can change drastically according to climate and season. The taste will be special from the very first, even if the dough seems thick or not kneaded well enough. With time, the cook will realize greater and greater perfection.

Probably the most important single quality in the finished pasta is the elasticity of the dough. As you work and knead the dough, experience will give you an almost instinctive knowledge of when the dough has reached the moment to roll. It should be shiny and smooth, and roll out slowly but evenly, without breaking. (With the handcrank machine, a lot of conjecture can be eliminated; you simply roll it out again and again until the perfect consistency and elasticity have been achieved.)

Determining the correct thickness is also made easier by the machine. Nevertheless, it can certainly be done by hand as well. Homemade pasta should simply be as thin as possible - not transparent, not difficult to manage, but thin.

If you don't have a little machine, you'll want a long, tapered skinny rolling pin, and a large wooden or formica surface to work on. The flour is heaped, the eggs, salt and oil dropped into a well, and the dough worked from there. Here are the amounts for an ample lasagne, a good serving of stuffed pasta, or noodles for six.

PLAIN PASTA

INGREDIENTS:
2¹/₂-3 cups all-purpose flour
3 whole eggs (or, for a lighter dough, 2 eggs, and 2 tablespoons water), lightly beaten together with a fork
A good pinch of salt
1 tablespoon olive oil

1. Sift the flour onto a large clean surface, gather into a heap and make a well in the center. Drop the eggs, salt and olive oil into the well, and work together into a paste.

2. Flour your hands and begin to work the dough, using the heel of your hand and flattening the dough as you work. Gather it again and again into a ball, and push it out again and again. Add flour as you work, both on the surface and on your hands. The dough will become less and less sticky and eventually should be entirely pliable and fairly soft.

3. Work the dough in this way for about 10 minutes, or until it is shiny smooth and pulls out without tearing. Roll into a ball, cover with a cloth or an overturned casserole and allow it to rest for 10-15 minutes. (In very dry air, dampen the cloth a bit.)

4. Divide the dough into halves or thirds, and begin to roll out. If using a handcranked machine, run dough through the broadest thickness. Run it again and again, each time reducing the width until, for the final rolling, the machine is set to its thinnest width. The dough is then cut according to desired size, through cutters adapted to the machine.

If using a rolling pin, begin to roll out the dough gently but firmly, turning with each roll to form a circle. Continue the motion until the dough has been rolled down to about 1/2 inch thickness. For the final rolling, dust the surface of the dough with flour. Roll the sheet of dough on the rolling pin, pressing and working the pin back and forth to create the thinnest dough possible. At the same time, work the dough outwards with your hands toward the ends of the rolling pin, widening it as you lengthen it with the rolling pin itself, until it is as thin as you desire. Slowly, wrap the dough entirely around the pin; slip out the rolling pin and, with a very sharp knife, slice the dough into the desired widths.

When making fresh noodles, unravel the cut slices, separate and allow them to dry over the back of a chair or on a well-floured surface.

Recipes for sauces to use with fresh pasta can be found throughout the book. Almost any sauce can be used, although light tomato, simple olive oil or butter and herb sauces are the best complements.

Stuffed pasta doughs are prepared in much the same way. You can add a teaspoon of milk to the dough to make it easier to seal. After the final rolling, however, the dough is laid flat, cut and filled according to the desired shape.

Filling the pasta is also something that experience will perfect. You'll want enough filling for character, but not so much that the pasta will looked overstuffed, or that the filling will seep through the sealed edges. A scant teaspoon is the rule. The pasta should be filled quickly, before the dough dries too much to be sealed effectively.

As a first stuffed pasta, I would suggest trying small round ravioli shapes. They can be filled, cut with a cookie cutter or sharp-edged glass and sealed easily. Or the same round shape - with somewhat less filling - can be folded in half to form a half-moon shape. The dough is worked a little at a time, cut, filled and sealed, with the unrolled remainder waiting under a damp cloth. The pastas are pinched between the thumb and forefinger all around to seal, then laid on a floured cloth to dry, as you work with another batch of dough.

The little squares of *ravioli* are made in a slightly different way. Here, one rectangular layer of dough (much like *a lasagne* layer) is spread out, little mounds of filling placed at proper intervals, the second layer of dough placed over the first, squares are cut out with a pastry or pizza cutter and sealed between the fingers. (There is a little rectangular table device for making a quantity of these small squares at a single time, with indentations for filling; I have never found it very helpful.)

Other filled pastas require a bit more dexterity and practice: the *tortellini* and *cappelletti* (little hats), which begin as circles *(tortellini)* or squares *(cappelletti),* then filled, folded and wrapped around one's finger to make little caps or dumplings.

Stuffed pasta recipes, with suggested sauces, are below.

BROAD (FAVA) BEAN FILLING

A bit of a bother to double peel the broad beans, but the taste and texture are well worth it: sweet and succulent.

INGREDIENTS:
1¹/₂ lbs. fresh broad beans, unpeeled
1¹/₂ tablespoons butter
3 leaves light green lettuce, cut in strips
2 large eggs
¹/₄ cup grated Parmesan
Salt and freshly ground pepper

1. Take the beans from their pods, and pour over some boiling water. This will help to slip out the inner bean from its heavier shell. Remove inner skins - you should end up with about 10¹/₂ ounces of beans.

2. Melt the butter in a saute pan, and gently saute the beans for half an hour, with the lettuce strips. Add a bit of water every now and again to keep them cooking gently. When the beans are tender, remove them to a food processor, and blend to a puree. Transfer to a bowl, and allow to cool.

3. Add the eggs, half the cheese, salt and pepper. Fill the pasta, seal, and cook in a large amount of boiling salted water. Drain well, and serve with the following sauce.

SPRING ONION SAUCE

INGREDIENTS:
2 spring onions, sliced into ¹/₂ inch lengths
¹/₄ cup butter
¹/₄ cup grated Parmesan cheese

1. Saute the onions gently in the butter and pour the sauce over the pasta. Add salt and freshly ground pepper to taste, and mix well. Sprinkle with the grated Parmesan.

GNOCCHI DI PATATE

(Potato Gnocchi)

The simplest to make and most versatile of all gnocchi, these are little oval dumplings pressed with the tine of a fork (or, in Florence, against a cheese grater) to form a design. If you make them yourself, they look uneven and interesting, crafted by hand, which makes the serving that much more impressive.

A few things to remember:

1. Use boiling potatoes, but not new young ones.

2. Steam, rather than boil, the potatoes in their jackets and peel after; this prevents them absorbing too much moisture and will necessitate less flour

3. The final dough should be soft and malleable, and not sticky. Use as little extra flour as possible to make this so.

4. Gnocchi should be cooked in simmering, rather than violently boiling water. I like to drop them into boiling water, let the water boil up and immediately reduce the flame to simmer. Don't cook too many at once, and drop them into the hot sauce as soon as they surface.

INGREDIENTS:
1 lb. potatoes
2 teaspoons salt
A good grating of nutmeg
1-1½ cups flour

1. Steam the potatoes in their jackets until they are very soft. Allow to cool, peel and mash through a ricer or grate through the large holes of the food processor grater.

2. Put the potatoes in a large bowl, or on a floured surface, add about two teaspoons of salt and some nutmeg, and begin to add the flour, about ¼ cup at a time. The amount of flour you will need depends very much upon the moisture in the potatoes, and the weather. In humid conditions, you will undoubtedly need more flour.

3. Work the flour into the potatoes with a spoon or your hands, but do not expect it to be completely dry when you finish. The floured surface on which you roll it into a sausage shape will help to make the dough more malleable. Allow the dough to rest for an hour or two before proceeding. This allows the amalgamation of the flour with the potatoes.

4. Roll the dough out into thin sausage shapes about the width of a finger, a small amount at a time, and cut the sausages into 1 inch pieces. Press each of the sliced gnocchi with the tines of a fork, giving it a slightly ribbed look. Lay the gnocchi on a floured surface, until you have used up all of the dough.

5. Bring a wide pan of salted water to the boil, and drop in the gnocchi. Allow them to rise to the surface and cook for a minute, before removing with a slotted spoon into a warm serving dish.

6. Serve with melted butter, or a light tomato sauce. Pour the sauce over the gnocchi immediately and serve with cheese at the table.

GNOCCHI DI RICOTTA E SPINACI

The same combination that fills ravioli can be used with different proportions and the addition of flour to make delicious gnocchi. Frozen spinach works best; it has a finer consistency than fresh. Just make sure it is as dry as possible. Use a simple butter and cheese condiment.

INGREDIENTS:

1 package frozen spinach (about 1 lb.)
2 eggs
1 cup ricotta (8 oz.)
2 teaspoons salt
$^1/_4$ nutmeg, grated, or $^1/_4$ teaspoon ground
3 tablespoons grated Parmesan
Flour as needed (about $^1/_2$-1 cup)
2 tablespoons butter

1. Cook the spinach without water until it has thawed. Drain, and when cool, squeeze it to rid it of as much water as possible, and chop finely. Put in a warm oven to dry even more.

2. Beat the eggs to a foam in a mixing bowl, and add the ricotta, spinach, salt, nutmeg, and 1 tablespoon of the Parmesan. Blend thoroughly.

3. Add flour by the handful, mixing as you go, until the batter reaches the consistency of a workable paste. The amount of flour will depend upon the amount of liquid still in the spinach.

4. Allow the batter to rest for a few hours. Boil a large pan of salted water. Scoop up a teaspoonful of the batter, and roll into a little dumpling between your palms. Place each dumpling on a floured surface as you work.

5. Preheat the oven to warm (250^0 F.), and melt the butter in a small saucepan. As the water boils, lower it to simmer, and drop in the gnocchi, a few at a time. As the gnocchi rise to the top of the water, remove with a slotted spoon and transfer to a wide casserole.

6. When all the gnocchi have been cooked and are snug in the casserole, sprinkle over the remaining cheese, pour over the butter and keep warm until ready to serve. (Not too long!)

GNOCCHI DI ZUCCHINE

(Zucchini Gnocchi)

These gnocchi are best made with the aid of a pastry bag. It keeps them light and fluffy.

INGREDIENTS:

$1^1/_2$ lbs. small, firm zucchini
1 egg, lightly beaten
3 tablespoons finely grated Parmesan
Flour (about $^3/_4$ cup)
Tomato sauce (see Chapter 7)
Additional grated cheese

1. Steam the zucchini for about 20 minutes until just cooked. Slice lengthwise and remove the inner seed pockets, discard the seeds and finely chop the zucchini pulp. Place in a strainer or colander and press, to drain as much of the water as possible.

2. Put the zucchini in a bowl, and add the egg, grated cheese, and enough flour to make a good dry paste. Season with salt and pepper to taste, mix well and place the entire mass into a pastry bag with a wide nozzle.

3. Fill a pan with lightly salted water and bring to a boil. Reduce heat and allow water to simmer gently. Squeeze the gnocchi out of the pastry bag and slice them off in 2 inch cylinder shapes directly into the simmering water. Scoop them out as soon as they rise to the surface. Lightly cover with a plain tomato sauce, and serve with cheese at the table.

Note: If you do not have a pastry bag, shape the gnocchi into small ovals, 2 inches in length.

OLIVE OIL, HERBS
AND
PASTA COOKING

CHAPTER SIX

OLIVE OIL AND GARLIC

The simplest of condiments to prepare while the pasta is boiling. If six cloves of garlic seem too potent, use fewer. Be sure to eliminate all the stems from the parsley leaves; it makes for a much pleasanter feeling. It's important to use the best fresh olive oil available.

INGREDIENTS:
1 lb. spaghettini or other pasta
6 cloves garlic
1/2 cup fruity fresh olive oil
Salt and at least 10 grindings of pepper
1 small bunch parsley leaves, finely chopped

1. Peel and slice each clove of garlic fairly thickly, about five slices per clove.

2. Heat garlic slices and olive oil together in a heavy skillet over a medium fire. The garlic can either be left in the oil to be eaten together with the spaghetti, or removed when it turns light brown. Do not allow the garlic to burn; the taste can seem acrid, and is entirely different from that of a golden brown, gently sauteed garlic clove.

3. Cook the pasta in a large amount of well-salted boiling water (see pasta cooking instructions, Chapter 3), and drain into a heated serving dish. Pour the heated garlic oil over immediately, and mix thoroughly. Add salt and freshly ground pepper, sprinkle over the chopped parsley leaves, and mix well again before serving. Cheese is optional.

SPAGHETTI PROFUMATI

(Olive Oil and Mixed Herbs)

A combination of herbs and fresh olive oil that can be diversified as you see fit, depending upon the available herbs.

INGREDIENTS:
1 lb. spaghetti, or any other pasta
2 garlic cloves
1 bunch parsley leaves, finely chopped
1 bunch basil leaves, finely chopped
2 sprigs mint leaves, finely chopped
2 sprigs marjoram, finely chopped
1/2 cup olive oil
1 little hot chili pepper (peperoncino)
1/3 cup grated Parmesan cheese
Salt and freshly ground pepper

1. Cook pasta in lots of boiling salted water until *al dente* (see cooking instructions, Chapter 3). Meanwhile, mix garlic and all herbs together in a bowl.

2. In a separate pan, heat the oil with the *peperoncino*, and when it is hot, put in the herbs. Mix well and remove immediately from the flame.

3. Drain the pasta into a heated serving dish, without shaking (leaving the pasta somewhat dripping with water), pour over the herb mixture, mix well and add the grated Parmesan, salt and freshly ground pepper. Serve immediately.

see p.57

TOMATOES
AND
TOMATO SAUCES

CHAPTER SEVEN

POMMAROLA: BASIC TOMATO SAUCE

(Long-Cooking)

This is the sauce that Italians bottle when tomatoes are at their ripest, for an entire winter's use. The odori or aromatic vegetables are simmered together with the tomatoes - no oil is necessary - until most liquid has been eliminated. The entire potful is then put through the smallest holes of a food mill. It's the perfect summer sauce as well. The recipe is enough sauce for a little more than 1 pound of pasta.

INGREDIENTS:
2 lbs. fresh, ripe tomatoes, cut into quarters,
  or 1 large can of crushed, skinned plum tomatoes
1 medium carrot, coarsely chopped
1 medium onion, coarsely chopped
1 stalk celery, sliced
2 cloves garlic, peeled and halved
Salt
Leaves of one small bunch parsley

1. Put all the ingredients together into a heavy saucepan, and cook over lively heat for about 20 minutes, stirring every now and then as the tomatoes release their water. Reduce the flame, and cook slowly for another hour or 1 1/2 hours, uncovered, until most of the water has evaporated.

2. Put the entire contents of the saucepan through a food mill, straining out the skin and seeds, and store until ready to use. When reheating for sauce, add any herbs you might have fresh, and serve with a good helping of grated Parmesan cheese at the table.

TOMATO SAUCE WITH STOCK

(Long-cooking)

INGREDIENTS:
1/4 cup olive oil
2 tablespoons butter
1 onion, coarsely chopped
1 stalk celery, thinly sliced
1 carrot, coarsely chopped
1 small bunch parsley leaves
1 clove garlic, crushed
1/4 cup hot broth
2 lbs. fresh ripe tomatoes, cut into quarters,
  or 1 large can of crushed plum tomatoes
Salt and freshly ground pepper

1. Heat the oil, butter, chopped onion, celery, carrot, parsley and garlic in a deep heavy saucepan. As the vegetables just begin to brown, add the hot broth and cook over a low flame for five minutes.

2. Add the tomatoes, cover the pan and cook over a medium heat for 15 minutes. Uncover the pan, and continue to cook over a medium flame for 1 to 1 1/2 hours. Taste and add salt and a good bit of freshly ground pepper.

3. Put the sauce through the smallest holes of a food mill, or puree and strain. When reheating, add any fresh herb you might have on hand, and serve on a pasta with grated Parmesan cheese at the table.

GARLICKY NEAPOLITAN TOMATO SAUCE

The spices of Naples: lots of garlic and oregano added to barely cooked tomatoes. Quick and tasty.

INGREDIENTS
2 lbs. fresh ripe tomatoes, chopped, or the contents of 1 large
  can of plum tomatoes, drained and chopped
1/2 cup olive oil
4 cloves garlic, crushed
Leaves of 5 sprigs fresh basil, chopped
Leaves of 10 sprigs fresh parsley, chopped
1 heaping tablespoon oregano
Salt and fresh pepper to taste

1. Put the chopped tomatoes into a colander to drain. In a deep heavy saucepan, put the oil and crushed garlic. Turn on a medium flame. When the oil around the garlic begins to bubble, add the chopped tomatoes, the basil and parsley and cook together for fifteen minutes.

2. Add the oregano, salt and freshly ground pepper to taste, and keep warm until the pasta is cooked. Serve with grated Parmesan at the table.

TOMATO SAUCE WITH ROSEMARY AND SAUSAGE

Next time you find a fragrant sprig of rosemary, try using it to flavor a tomato pasta sauce. The recipe below is an example; remember that a little rosemary goes a long way.

INGREDIENTS:
2 lbs. ripe fresh tomatoes, or the
  contents of 1 large can of chopped
  plum tomatoes
2 carrots, coarsely chopped
1 onion, coarsely chopped
1 stalk celery, sliced

1/3 cup olive oil
2 teaspoons rosemary leaves,
  finely chopped
2 ounces salami, thinly sliced
  and cut into fine strips
Salt and freshly ground pepper

1. If using fresh tomatoes, place them in a bowl, pour over boiling water, slip off the skins, halve and squeeze to remove all seeds and juices. Halve again and drain in a colander. If using canned chopped tomatoes, use the entire contents.

2. Combine the carrots, onion, celery and tomatoes with a good amount of salt in a heavy, non-stick saucepan, cook rapidly for about 15 minutes, until the tomatoes give off their water, lower the flame and cook uncovered for about 1/2 hour, until the vegetables are soft.

3. Puree the tomato sauce, and return to pan.

4. Put the oil, rosemary and salami strips in a small frying pan, and fry together over a medium flame for 2 minutes, stirring constantly.

5. Pour the contents of the frying pan into the tomato puree, and cook together for another fifteen minutes. Taste and correct for salt, and add lots of freshly ground pepper.

TOMATO SAUCE
WITH BEEF

(Long Cooking)

This sauce has just a bit of minced meat that later gets pureed with the vegetables into a thick sauce. A few dried mushrooms can enrich the taste as well.

INGREDIENTS:

A handful dried porcini mushrooms
$^1/_3$ cup olive oil
1 onion, coarsely chopped
1 carrot, coarsely chopped
1 stalk celery, sliced
2 cloves garlic, crushed

$3^1/_2$ ounces chopped meat
(or small bit of leftover, minced)
2 lbs. fresh ripe tomatoes, cut into
quarters, or 1 large can of
chopped plum tomatoes
Salt and freshly ground pepper

1. Soak the mushrooms in warm water for about $^1/_2$ hour. Remove the mushrooms, strain the water through a paper towel and set aside.

2. Put the oil, onion, carrot, celery and garlic into a heavy deep saucepan, heat together over a medium flame and saute until the onion is transparent.

3. Add the chopped meat and continue to fry, mashing with a fork, until the meat has lost its redness. Add the mushrooms and the strained water, and continue to cook until the water has evaporated.

4. Add the tomatoes, bring the sauce to a boil, reduce the flame and simmer for 1 to $1^1/_2$ hours. Put the sauce through a food mill, taste and season with salt and freshly ground pepper, and re-heat before using.

TOMATO SAUCE WITH BUTTER AND ONION

This sauce is pure tomato, with the enhancement of only an onion and butter. The onion is discarded before serving.

INGREDIENTS:
*2 lbs. ripe fresh tomatoes, quartered, or the contents
  of 1 large can of crushed plum tomatoes
1/2 cup butter
1 onion, halved
1/2 teaspoon sugar
Salt and freshly ground pepper*

1. Put the tomatoes into a deep saucepan over a high flame. When their water has been released and begins to bubble, reduce the flame and cook for ten minutes. Remove from fire and puree through a food mill to remove seeds and skin. Return to pan.

2. Add the butter and onion halves to the pan, together with the sugar and some of salt, and cook over a low flame for about an hour, uncovered. The sauce should reduce to a creamy consistency.

3. Remove the onion before serving. Taste for seasoning, and serve the pasta with grated Parmesan cheese.

TOMATO SAUCE WITH FRESH HERBS

Marjoram is available both as a plant and at greengrocers; this sauce calls for quite a bit, and has a full aroma. If you don't find it, another fresh herb - thyme or oregano especially - will suffice, but it's worth seeking out even wild marjoram to make this sauce.

INGREDIENTS:
*2 lbs. ripe fresh tomatoes, or 1
  large and 1 small can of skinned
  plum tomatoes
2 carrots, coarsely chopped
1 onion, coarsely chopped
2 stalks celery, coarsely chopped
1/3 cup olive oil
Leaves of 3 stalks marjoram,
  chopped
Salt and freshly ground pepper.
2 tablespoons grated Parmesan
  cheese*

1. If using fresh tomatoes, put them in a bowl, pour over boiling water, and eliminate the skins. Slice them in quarters, and squeeze to remove all seeds and water within. Drain in a colander. If using canned tomatoes, remove them from their juice, halve and discard the seeds within. Halve again, and drain in a colander.

2. Put the tomatoes in a saucepan, add the chopped carrots, celery and onion with a teaspoon of salt and cook together slowly, over a low flame, uncovered, for half an hour, or until the vegetables are completely soft. Remove from flame, and blend.

3. Return the puree to the pan, add a generous grinding of fresh pepper, the olive oil and the marjoram and simmer over a low flame for another 10 minutes before serving over a pasta, with the grated Parmesan on the side.

SALSA CRUDA I

INGREDIENTS:

2 lbs. fresh ripe tomatoes, skinned, seeded, drained and finely chopped
1/3 cup olive oil
10 leaves fresh basil, finely chopped
Leaves of 10 sprigs parsley, finely chopped
1/4 cup grated Parmesan
Freshly ground pepper
Salt (add just before serving)

SALSA CRUDA II

INGREDIENTS:

2 lbs. fresh ripe tomatoes, skinned, seeded, drained and finely chopped
1/3 cup olive oil
2 spring onions, finely chopped with as much of the green as edible.
1 bunch parsley leaves, finely chopped
1 clove garlic, crushed
Freshly ground pepper
Salt (add just before serving)

SALSA CRUDA III

INGREDIENTS:

2 lbs. fresh ripe tomatoes, skinned, seeded, drained and finely chopped
1/2 sweet red onion, finely chopped
1 tablespoon dried oregano, rubbed in through the palms.
1/3 cup olive oil
Freshly ground pepper
Salt (add just before serving)

SALSA CRUDA IV

INGREDIENTS:

2 lbs. fresh ripe tomatoes, skinned, seeded, drained and finely chopped
1/3 cup olive oil
2 tablespoons fresh oregano, chopped well.
1 clove garlic, crushed
Freshly ground pepper
Salt (add just before serving)

Salsa Cruda VIII, p.54

SPAGHETTI UBRIACHI

(Drunken Spaghetti)

The bath of white wine gives this pasta its enticing name. The pasta is drained while it still needs some cooking, and finishes in the garlic-flavored oil and wine. For the sober diner, it has a nice tang, a good garlic taste and a bit of spicy interest as well.

INGREDIENTS:
1 lb. spaghettini, fedelini or other long thin pasta
$1/3$ cup olive oil
3 cloves garlic, peeled and halved
1 little piece of hot chili pepper
1 cup dry white wine
Salt
1 bunch basil, finely chopped
1 bunch parsley, finely chopped
$1/3$ cup grated Parmesan cheese

1. In a flameproof serving dish that can later hold all the pasta, heat the olive oil together with the garlic and hot chili, until the garlic begins to brown. At this point, mash the garlic down with a fork and remove.

2. Add the wine and some salt, and bring to the boil. Allow to boil for three minutes, and turn off the flame.

3. Boil the pasta in a large amount of salted water. When not quite *al dente*, still a bit tough, drain and shake it dry in the colander.

4. Turn on a small flame under the oil-wine mixture, and drop in the pasta, mixing constantly to make sure all the pasta gets the bath. When the oil-wine is almost absorbed, add the chopped basil, the chopped parsley and the grated cheese. Mix well and serve immediately.

PAGLIA E FIENO

(Straw & Hay)

Paglia e Fieno means "straw and hay", which, for this particular pasta at least can be interpreted as green and white (or white and green). It's a mixture of broad green and white noodles - fettuccine or tagliatelle - if at all possible, fresh (for homemade and fresh pastas, see Chapter 5). A most elegant first course.

INGREDIENTS:

7 oz. fresh white fettuccine noodles, either store-bought or homemade
7 oz. fresh green fettuccine noodles, either store-bought or homemade
4 tablespoons butter
1 shallot, finely chopped
1 lb. fresh crisp champignon mushrooms, wiped clean and thinly sliced
Salt and freshly ground pepper
3/4 cup fresh or frozen peas, thawed (about 5 oz. shelled weight)
1 cup fresh cream
1/3 cup freshly grated Parmesan

1. In a deep large skillet, melt the butter and add the shallot. Saute until just transparent.

2. Turn the heat to high, add the mushrooms and and saute quickly, just until they have absorbed the butter. Turn down the heat, add salt and lots of freshly ground pepper and continue to cook just until the mushrooms begin to give out water.

3. Add the peas and cook for a minute. Pour in the cream, bring to a boiling point, and cook just long enough for the sauce to thicken, about five minutes.

4. Bring a large pot of salted water to boil, and drop in the pasta, green first, and a minute later the regular. Cook until just *al dente* (see cooking instructions, Chapter 3), drain and transfer to a heated serving dish. Pour over the sauce, mix well, and add more pepper and the cheese on top. Serve immediately, with more cheese if you like at the table.

SPAGHETTI DEL CASARO

(Cheesemaker's Spaghetti)

I have no idea of either the origin of this particular pasta or the reason it is attributed to the cheesemaker. But it is worth recording, if only for the spray of fresh wild fennel leaves that goes over the top (wild fennel looks like dill, but is definitely not the same). It's a pasta to serve when fields are filled with wild fennel and the tomatoes are at the most vine-ripened fullness.

INGREDIENTS:

1 lb. spaghetti or other long pasta
4 tablespoons olive oil
2 cloves garlic, pressed
1 lb. fresh firm ripe tomatoes, skinned, seeded, drained and chopped
1 small chili pepper
Salt and freshly ground pepper
9 oz. ricotta cheese, broken to pieces at the last minute
1 large bunch wild fennel leaves, chopped
1/4 cup grated Parmesan cheese

1. In a large heavy sauce pan, heat the oil together with the pressed garlic until the oil around the garlic begins to bubble. Add the tomatoes and the small hot pepper, a generous teaspoon of salt and some good gratings of pepper, and allow to cook for about 10 minutes, until the tomatoes have begun to give off their water.

2. Cook the pasta in a large pot of boiling salted water until just *al dente* (see cooking instructions, Chapter 3). Drain and transfer to a heated serving dish.

3. Pour over the sauce, and on top add the ricotta, broken up into small pieces, the chopped fennel leaves, and half the grated cheese. Mix well, and serve with the remaining grated cheese at the table.

VEGETABLE
PASTA
SAUCES

PASTA WITH EGGPLANT

Eggplant and pasta marry wonderfully. The sensuous, deep purple vegetable (more correctly, fruit) has the flavor and feel of the Mediterranean, especially when combined with garlic and olive oil, and herbs. Eggplant goes well with tomatoes too, and, when properly handled, can yield a most soothing, even elegant taste.

It is not a vegetable one thinks of immediately when considering what to put over a pasta, but oddly enough, eggplant pastas are in great demand in our home. An eggplant pasticcio is a favorite with children; one with lasagne has served for many successful dinner parties. Both recipes are in Chapter 13.

A most important rule in dealing with eggplant - no matter what its size or color - is that the bitter juices be removed before you begin. After it is sliced (preferably lengthwise, for whatever reason) or chopped, salt the pieces liberally and leave them to drip in a colander for at least half an hour, or lie in the sun, where the water quickly evaporates. Squeeze the slices dry through a paper towel and proceed with the recipe; the taste is vastly improved.

SPAGHETTI CON MELANZANE E PEPERONI

(Spaghetti with Eggplant and Peppers)

A full and nourishing pasta that can serve as a one course dinner for six, with only the addition of salad, fruit and cheese. It's also a pleasing and colorful dish to present. The sauce can be prepared well beforehand, and reheated while the pasta is cooking.

INGREDIENTS:
1 lb. spaghetti or other long pasta
1 large eggplant
3 red peppers, or a mixture of red and yellow - not green
¼ cup olive oil
1 small celery root (about 2 oz.), finely chopped
1 carrot, finely chopped
1 lb. fresh ripe tomatoes, skinned, seeded and chopped (see method, Chapter 7), or the contents of 1 small can of crushed plum tomatoes
1 small bunch parsley, finely chopped
Salt and freshly ground pepper
Grated Parmesan cheese (optional)

1. Without peeling the eggplant, slice it first lengthwise, and then into fairly thick strips, somewhat like oversized matchsticks. Salt them liberally and allow to drain for at least half an hour. Rinse, squeeze out the excess juice and dry well.

2. Split the peppers, remove seeds and ribs, and slice into similar strips.

3. In a large deep pan heat the olive oil over a medium flame. When hot, add all at once the eggplant, the peppers, the chopped celery and carrot, and cook quickly, stirring all the while.

4. After about five minutes of cooking, add the tomatoes, bring to a boil and reduce the flame. Cover and cook slowly for 30 minutes. Add the parsley, salt to taste and about 10 grindings of fresh pepper. Keep warm while the pasta cooks.

5. Cook the spaghetti in a large pan of boiling salted water (see cooking method, Chapter 3), drain and transfer to a heated serving dish. Pour the sauce over, mix well and serve with the optional grated Parmesan at the table.

SPAGHETTI CON MELANZANE E FORMAGGI

(Spaghetti with Eggplant and Cheese)

This recipe calls for peeled eggplant. Peeling is not absolutely necessary, but the final texture will be somewhat more delicate.

INGREDIENTS:

1 lb. spaghetti or other long pasta
1 large eggplant, or two small ones (about 1¹/₂ lbs.)
Light oil for frying
¹/₄ cup olive oil
1 medium onion, finely chopped
4 cloves garlic, crushed
2 lbs. fresh ripe tomatoes, skinned, seeded and chopped (see Method, Chapter 7), or 1 large can crushed plum tomatoes, with their juice
Salt and freshly ground pepper
2 tablespoons (1 oz.) ricotta cheese
¹/₄ cup milk
1 bunch basil leaves, torn
1 small bunch parsley leaves, finely chopped
2 oz. mild Gruyere, grated
¹/₄ cup grated Parmesan cheese

1. Peel and dice the eggplant into large cubes. Sprinkle liberally with salt and place in a colander to drain for at least half an hour.

2. Rinse the eggplant cubes and squeeze dry. Heat the frying oil in a large heavy skillet, and fry cubes until tender and golden. Remove with a slotted spoon and drain on paper towels.

3. Pour off the frying oil from the skillet and add the olive oil, the onion and crushed garlic. Stir-fry for a few minutes until the onion is transparent and add the tomatoes. Bring to a boil and cook for five minutes, stirring frequently.

4. Add the fried eggplant to the tomatoes, mix well and continue to cook over a lowered flame for another two minutes. Season to taste with salt and some grindings of fresh pepper. Keep warm over a minimal flame.

5. Put the pasta to cook in a large pan of boiling salted water (see cooking method, Chapter 3). When *al dente*, drain and transfer to a heated serving dish.

6. Mash the ricotta with the milk, add to the sauce, mix and pour over the pasta. Mix well, add the torn basil and chopped parsley leaves, sprinkle over the combined grated cheeses and mix again before serving.

SPAGHETTI WITH ZUCCHINI AND DILL

Dill is practically unknown in Italy, but this pasta quickly became a favorite among our friends and family. Both zucchini and dill are often on hand; you'll find yourself, as I have, making it often.

INGREDIENTS:

1 lb. spaghetti or other pasta
1/2 cup butter
2 lbs. young firm zucchini, sliced into thin disks
1 full bunch of dill, finely chopped
Salt and freshly ground pepper

1. Gently melt the butter in a heavy saute pan, and add the zucchini before it has finished bubbling. Saute only for about three minutes; the zucchini should remain crisp. Add salt to taste.

2. Add the finely chopped dill, mix well into the zucchini and cook for another minute.

3. Cook the pasta in a large amount of boiling salted water until just *al dente* (see cooking instructions, Chapter 3), drain and transfer into a heated serving dish, reserving a ladle of the water in which the pasta was cooked.

4. Add the zucchini/dill mixture to the spaghetti, along with a few tablespoons of the cooking water, mix well and add freshly ground pepper. Serve immediately with more pepper at the table, and perhaps some grated Parmesan.

FUSILLI ALLA PAPOOSE

(Fusilli with Zucchini Cream Sauce)

This is another creamy zucchini sauce; but the creaminess here derives from a light bechamel base. The sauce goes well with the short spiral-shaped pasta, called fusilli, or corkscrew pasta. Zucchini are cut into short matchstick-length shapes. For best results with this sauce, prepare it at the very last minute, just before you are ready to begin your meal. The zucchini should remain crisp, and the sauce fresh.

INGREDIENTS:

1 lb. fusilli (corkscrew), or other short pasta
2 lbs. small, young, firm zucchini
Oil (preferably light olive) for frying
1 bunch dill
1/3 cup butter
4 tablespoons olive oil
1 teaspoon flour
2/3 cup milk
1 egg, well beaten
1/4 cup Parmesan cheese, grated
1/4 cup Gruyere cheese, grated
Salt and freshly ground pepper

1. Prepare the zucchini - if they are small, young and firm, do not peel - slice into matchstick-like lengths. If the zucchini are fat and blemished, peel, quarter lengthwise,and remove the seed pods, before slicing into the shorter lengths. Heat the frying oil in a frying pan and fry the zucchini, a handful at a time, until they are golden brown. Drain on absorbent paper.

2. Prepare dill - remove stems, and roughly chop leaves. Set aside.

3. In another deep saucepan, place half the butter together with the olive oil. Heat, and when the butter melts, add the flour and mix well. Slowly add the milk, stirring all the while, until the sauce thickens. Salt to taste, and add the zucchini. Add the dill, heat thoroughly, mix well and turn off the flame.

4. Add the remaining butter to the hot sauce, then add the egg and two types of cheeses. Taste, and correct seasoning for salt. The sauce should be quite seasoned, and of a light, creamy consistency. Keep the sauce warm while pasta is cooking.

5. Boil the pasta in a large amount of salted water until just *al dente* (see cooking instructions, Chapter 3). Drain immediately, transfer to a heated serving dish, pour the sauce over, mix well and serve.

SPAGHETTINI CON UOVA E ZUCCHINE

(Spaghettini with Creamy Egg Zucchini Sauce)

Beaten, uncooked eggs, added to the pasta before the zucchini, make this dish into a creamy succulent pasta

INGREDIENTS:

*1 lb. spaghettini, fedelini, or any
  other thin long pasta*
2 lbs. young firm zucchini, thinly sliced
2 tablespoons olive oil
1/4 cup butter

1 onion, finely chopped
2 eggs, well beaten
Salt and freshly ground pepper
1/4 cup grated Parmesan cheese

1. If the zucchini are small, young and firm, slice them into the thinnest slices possible. If they are fat and blemished, peel, quarter lengthwise and remove the seed pods before slicing thinly. Lightly salt slices and leave in a colander to drain for a few minutes.

2. In a deep heavy saucepan, put the oil and butter together with the chopped onion. Cook over a low flame until the onion becomes transparent. Add the zucchini, turn the flame up a bit, and brown gently. Keep warm.

3. Put pasta to cook in a large amount of salted boiling water (see cooking instructions, Chapter 3) until just *al dente*.

4. While pasta is cooking, beat the two eggs well with a half teaspoon of salt, in the bowl in which you plan to serve the pasta. Add the cheese and mix well again.

5. Drain the pasta quickly and, while still steaming hot, add it to the egg mixture. Mix quickly with two forks, making sure each strand of pasta gets covered. Don't leave any egg mixture in the bottom of the serving dish, but continue to mix until it is all absorbed into the pasta.

6. Pour over the zucchini, mix again quickly and thoroughly, add another several good grindings of pepper, salt to taste and serve immediately.

CONCHIGLIE CON ZUCCHINE E BRANDY

(Shells with Zucchini and Brandy)

Another pasta that uses zucchini simmered in milk, this one with an added sweetness of brandy and a whisper of cinnamon and nutmeg that gives a most distinctive flavor. The pasta is finished in the sauce, which enriches it deliciously.

INGREDIENTS:

1 lb. conchiglie (pasta shells)
1 medium onion, finely chopped
2 cloves garlic, minced
1/4 teaspoon ground cinnamon
1/4 teaspoon grated nutmeg
Salt and freshly ground pepper
2 lbs. small zucchini, thinly sliced
1/4 cup brandy
1 tablespoon vegetable broth powder
1 1/2 cups skim milk
1/3 cup olive oil
1/3 cup grated Parmesan cheese
1 teaspoon butter

1. In a deep heavy saucepan, large enough to hold both the zucchini and pasta, put the onion, the garlic, the cinnamon and nutmeg, with a tablespoon or two of water, salt and some freshly ground pepper. Turn on the flame, and allow the onion to wilt in the water.

2. Add the sliced zucchini and brandy, mix well and allow to cook for a few minutes. Sprinkle over the broth powder, add the milk, bring to a boil, lower the heat and cook slowly for about 15 minutes, or until the zucchini are cooked.

3. Cook the shells in a large amount of boiling salted water (see cooking instructions, Chapter 3) until they are almost *al dente*. Drain, add to the zucchini, and mix well over a low flame. When the zucchini sauce is totally absorbed into the pasta, remove from flame, and mix in the oil, grated cheese and a teaspoon of butter. Serve immediately.

INGRID'S ZUCCHINI PASTA

With the addition of pine nuts and raisins, there is something of a Sicilian influence in this pasta, although I'm not sure that was the intention of my Milanese friend who created it. Her recipe insists upon capers preserved in salt.

INGREDIENTS:

1 lb. penne, or other short pasta
2 tablespoons raisins
10 garlic cloves, sliced
¹/₃ cup olive oil.
1 heaping tablespoon capers (if possible, preserved in salt), chopped
1 generous handful pine nuts
1 small chili pepper, chopped
1 lb. small zucchini, thinly sliced
1 bunch parsley leaves, chopped
1 bunch basil leaves, chopped
¹/₃ cup smoked Provolone cheese, grated

1. Put the raisins in a bowl, add hot water to cover and soak for an hour. Drain and set aside.

2. Put the sliced garlic and the oil into a deep heavy pot that can later hold the pasta. When the oil begins to bubble around the garlic, add the capers, fry for 1 minute then add the pine nuts, raisins and chili pepper. Add the zucchini and cook gently for about 15 minutes.

3. Add the chopped parsley. There should be a good bit of it. At the last minute, when the pasta is boiling. add the chopped basil, also a generous measure.

4. Boil a large amount of salted water and cook the pasta until just *al dente* (see cooking instructions, chapter 3). Just before the pasta is cooked, add a ladle or two of cooking water to the sauce. When pasta is done, drain and toss it into the cooking pot, together with the grated cheese. Mix together until all the water has disappeared and the pasta is well glazed with the sauce. Serve immediately.

BELL PEPPERS

Among the most appealing and tasty pastas are those that have a goodly amount of red and/or yellow bell peppers in the sauce. Together with a splash of green - be it parsley, basil, or another green vegetable - the contrasting colors can rouse even the most unenthusiastic diner. Generally I like to scorch and peel the peppers before making a sauce, a process which gives them a most delicate quality.

A tasty and easy way to blacken peppers is to put them - as many as will fit - on a small, flat grill laid over the flame atop the stove. In summer, an open barbecue fire is even better. Turn them quickly with a prong, just as soon as they bubble and blacken. This process blackens the peppers quickly without cooking them, while giving them a sweet smoky flavor. The peppers need watching, turning and some careful attention. The whole process can be somewhat messy, with peppers dripping their juices into the flame, but the results, I think, are the best. They peel easily under running water, or first can be stored for a few minutes in a closed paper sack. If you prefer to grill them in the oven, try not to let them cook, or get too soft. The microwave also does a good job, but you'll miss the nice flavor an open flame gives.

Green bell peppers have a taste of their own, which seems to me generally less satisfactory in pastas of the Mediterranean, but this may be a personal prejudice. I include below a Pasta Arcobaleno *(Rainbow Pasta) which uses a combination of all colors of peppers for those who favor green peppers as well. Unless the green peppers are of the dark green, sturdy variety, it's not very practical to blacken them; they wilt away into nothing.*

Here are a handful of sauces which feature peppers as a major ingredient. There will be other sauces that use peppers (see index) together with other vegetables later on in this chapter, and lots more in "pasticcios" in another chapter.

PENNE CON PEPERONI E FORMAGGIO

(Penne with Peperoni and Sweet Cheese)

Sweet red peppers in a sweet cheese sauce.

INGREDIENTS:

1 lb. penne or other short tubular pasta
3 red peppers, seeded, ribbed and finely diced
1/3 cup olive oil
5 oz. Gruyere, cut into small pieces.
1/4 cup milk
Handful fresh chopped chives
Salt and freshly ground pepper to taste

1. Put the diced peppers and olive oil into a deep saute pan, and cook over a medium flame for about 20 minutes, or until the peppers are soft.

2. Put the pasta to cook in a large amount of salted water until just *al dente* (see cooking instruction, Chapter 3).

3. While the pasta is cooking, add the cheese to the peppers, mix well, and add the milk to help the cheese melt into the peppers. If cheese seems to stick in a mass, add more milk. Warm thoroughly, season with salt and lots of freshly ground peppers, and mix to keep it all amalgamated while the pasta cooks. (Don't allow it to boil and separate)

4. Drain the pasta into a heated serving dish, pour the sauce over, mix well, sprinkle over a handful of chopped chives and serve.

SPAGHETTINI CON PEPERONI, MELANZANE E POMODORO

(Spaghettini with Peppers, Eggplant and Tomatoes)

This hearty pasta is a nice party dish, rich in slightly piquant tastes and lots of color. It looks most inviting in a plain white bowl. Gambas are those stout and fleshy red peppers that look like mini red pumpkins; if they are not handy, red and/or yellow bell peppers make a perfectly good substitute.

INGREDIENTS:

1 lb. spaghettini (thinnest spaghetti) or fedelini
1 small eggplant, diced (with skin) into small cubes
3 gambas, or 2 red bell peppers
¹/4 cup olive oil
2 cloves garlic, pressed
1 large can of plum tomatoes, seeded' drained of juices and coarsely chopped
1 oz. pitted black olives, halved
1 teaspoon capers, coarsely chopped
4 anchovy fillets, drained and chopped (optional)
1 small bunch basil leaves, chopped
Salt and freshly ground pepper to taste

1. Place the diced eggplant in a colander, salt liberally and drain for at least 1/2 hour. Squeeze dry.

2. Scorch the whole gambas over an open flame. Rub off the skin, cut in half to remove the seeds and inner ribs, and slice into strips 1/4 inch wide.

3. Put the oil and crushed garlic together in a heavy saucepan and heat over a medium flame. When the oil around the garlic begins to bubble, add the eggplant. Mix and fry for five to ten minutes, until the eggplant is browned.

4. Add the tomatoes, mix well and bring to a boil. Reduce the flame to moderate, cover and cook for another ten minutes.

5. Add the gamba strips, the olives and chopped anchovy fillets. Add salt to taste (about 1/2 teaspoon if not using anchovies, less if you are) and freshly ground pepper, cover again and cook for another fifteen minutes. Add the basil and keep warm while pasta is cooking.

6. Cook the spaghettini in a large pan of boiling salted water until just *al dente* (see cooking instructions, Chapter 3). Drain, transfer to a heated serving dish, pour over the sauce, mix well and serve, with a pepper grinder on the table.

PASTA ARCOBALENO

(Rainbow Pasta)

Red, green and yellow peppers dotted with black olives combine to give this tasty pasta its colorful name.

INGREDIENTS:
1 lb. spaghetti, bavette or bucatini
3 peppers, one red, one yellow, one fleshy dark green
1 small onion, finely chopped
2 cloves garlic, pressed
¹/₃ cup olive oil
2 stalks celery, finely sliced
1 heaping teaspoon vegetable broth powder
³/₄ cup boiling water
pinch of sharp paprika
¹/₄ cup (about 2 oz.) pitted black olives, halved
3 fillets of anchovy, drained of their oil, halved lengthwise and cut into thirds
Salt and pepper to taste

1. Burn the peppers over a flame until they are black. Skin them completely, halve them, eliminate the seeds and inner ribs and slice them into thin strips.

2. In a deep heavy saute pan, put the chopped onion and pressed garlic together with the oil. Heat for a few minutes over a lively flame, and add the sliced celery. Cook together for five minutes, and add the peppers. Cook for another minute.

3. Dissolve the broth powder in the boiling water and add to the pan, with the sharp paprika and a good bit of freshly ground pepper. Cook for another fifteen minutes. While the pasta is cooking, add the olives and anchovy fillets to the sauce. Keep warm while the pasta cooks.

4. Cook the pasta in lots of boiling salted water until just *al dente* (see cooking instructions, Chapter 3). Drain; transfer to a heated serving dish, moisten with a bit of olive oil and pour the sauce over. Mix well and serve.

SPAGHETTI CON BROCCOLI

(Spaghetti with Broccoli)

Both broccoli and cauliflower are popular vegetables for the Sicilian pasta sauce called Arriminata. Arriminata is an agrodolce (sweet-sour) sauce, using as it does a handful of raisins added to otherwise piquant ingredients. I've included several arriminata recipes in the book, including this one and another for zucchini (Ingrid's Zucchini Pasta). Still another, a pasticcio using broccoli, is included in the chapter on oven-baked pastas. The traditional Bucatini co' I Vruoccoli Arriminati (a name in Sicilian dialect) is included in pastas for cauliflower; it can be made with either broccoli or cauliflower.

INGREDIENTS:
1 lb. spaghetti
1 lb. broccoli
2 tablespoons sultana raisins
1/3 cup olive oil
2 cloves garlic, pressed
1 lb. fresh plum tomatoes, skinned, drained, seeded and chopped, or the contents of 1 small can of plum tomatoes, drained, seeded and chopped
1 small piece hot chili pepper
1 tablespoon pine nuts
1 small bunch parsley leaves, chopped
Salt and freshly ground pepper to taste

1. Separate flowerets from broccoli stems, and set aside. Peel stems, chop roughly and keep in a separate bowl. Boil salted water in a pan that can later cook the pasta, add the broccoli stems and cook for five minute. Drop in the flowerets and cook for for five or six more minutes, until tender. Remove with a slotted spoon and set aside.

2. Place raisins in a bowl, add hot water to cover and soak for an hour. Drain and set aside.

3. In a deep casserole, heat the olive oil together with the garlic until the oil around the garlic begins to bubble. Add the tomatoes, cook for a minute or two, then add the raisins and hot chili pepper. Allow to cook uncovered for fifteen minutes over a moderate flame. Add the pine nuts and the broccoli, mix well, and remove from flame. Add salt and freshly ground pepper to taste.

4. Cook the spaghetti in the broccoli water until just al dente (see cooking instructions, Chapter 3). Drain, transfer to a heated serving dish, mix in the sauce and the chopped parsley leaves, and serve.

BUCATINI ALLA BOSCAIOLA

(Bucatini with Mushrooms, Tomatoes and Herbs)

alla boscaiola *means "of the forest", and this savory sauce has just that taste. Lovely-looking oyster mushrooms, eggplant and tomatoes combine to create a fresh woodsy taste. The sage works best, but marjoram or oregano can serve if no fresh sage is available. Two heavy saucepans are required for the sauce; the contents are combined only at the last minute.*

INGREDIENTS:
1 lb. long bucatini noodles, or other long thick noodles
2 medium eggplants
¹/₂ lb. fresh oyster mushrooms
¹/₃ cup olive oil
3 garlic cloves, pressed
7 fresh sage leaves (or 2 sprigs marjoram,
  or 1 tablespoon dried oregano)
1 lb. ripe plum tomatoes, skinned, drained seeded and chopped,
  or the contents of 1 small can of plum tomatoes,
  drained of their juices, seeded and chopped
¹/₄ cup butter, at room temperature.
¹/₂ cup grated Parmesan cheese
Salt and freshly ground pepper

1. If the eggplants are undamaged and fresh, do not peel them. If they are slightly old and bruised, best to peel. Dice them into small cubes, sprinkle with salt and lay in a colander to drain for at least half an hour. Squeeze out excess liquid.

2. Wipe the mushrooms and slice into strips of about ¹/₄ inch width, if using oyster mushrooms, and thinly if using champignons.

3. In one heavy pan, heat half the olive oil together with the crushed garlic and sage (or marjoram). When the oil around the garlic begins to bubble, add the tomatoes. Cook for 20 minutes, and season liberally with salt and freshly ground pepper.

4. Put a large pan of salted water to boil for the pasta (see cooking instructions, Chapter 3).

5. Heat the remaining oil in a separate pan. Add the eggplant cubes and fry for ten minutes, or until they are cooked but not soggy. Add the sliced mushrooms, mix well and continue cooking for a few more minutes. Try not to overcook the mushrooms; they should remain firm.

6. When the pasta is *al dente,* drain and transfer to a heated serving dish. Mix the butter into the pasta with two forks. Mix in the tomato sauce, sprinkle over the grated cheese and mix again. Pour over the eggplant and mushrooms, mix again and serve immediately.

LUXURIOUS MUSHROOM PASTA

Mushrooms melted in a creamy brandied butter sauce over the thinnest of noodles is an impressive and filling dish. A green salad, cheese and some dessert is all the accompaniment necessary.

INGREDIENTS:

1 lb. spaghettini, fedelini, or any
  other long, thin pasta
4 onions, halved then sliced
  as thinly as possible
1/2 cup butter
1 lb. fresh mushrooms

2 tablespoons brandy
Salt and lots of freshly
  ground pepper.
Grating of nutmeg
1 cup fresh cream
1/4 cup grated Parmesan cheese

1. Put the onion slices and half the butter in a heavy pan. Saute gently until just transparent, cover the pan, lower the flame and cook the onions for 1/2 hour, until they are almost a puree. Check the onions as they cook; if they begin to dry, add a tablespoon or two of water.

2. Wipe the mushrooms clean with a damp cloth. If they are slightly discolored - not absolutely fresh - peel them instead. Slice thinly, along with as much of the stem as is fresh. Melt the remaining butter in a second frying pan and saute the mushrooms for a few minutes, until they are slightly cooked, but still firm.

3. Add the brandy to the mushrooms and allow to bubble for another minute. Add the mushrooms into the onion puree, mix well, add salt, lots of freshly ground pepper and the nutmeg. Up to this point, the recipe can be completed some hours before serving. Remove from flame, cover and reheat gently before adding the cream at the last minute.

4. Boil a large amount of salted water and cook the spaghettini until just *al dente* (see cooking instructions, Chapter 3). While the spaghettini are cooking, reheat the mushroom-onion mixture very gently, add the cream and heat just to the boiling point.

5. Drain the spaghettini, transfer to a heated serving dish, pour over the sauce, sprinkle on the grated cheese, and mix thoroughly before serving.

SPAGHETTINI CON FUNGHI E LIMONE

(Spaghettini with Mushroom and Lemon Sauce)

Lemony and light, this refreshing pasta dish makes a perfect first course for a light dinner. Its slightly sharp flavor is a nice change from what is usually expected in a pasta; other lemon sauces are included elsewhere.

INGREDIENTS:

1 lb. spaghettini, fedelini
  or any other long thin pasta
1 lb. smallest, firmest, freshest
  champignon mushrooms
1/4 cup plus 1 tablespoon butter
1/4 cup olive oil

Salt and freshly ground pepper
  to taste.
Juice of 2 large lemons
  (or less, depending on taste)
1 small bunch parsley leaves,
  finely chopped

1. Wipe the mushrooms clean and slice into fairly thin slices, including as much of the stem as looks fresh.

2. In a deep heavy skillet, melt 1/4 cup of butter into the olive oil. When the butter has melted, add the mushrooms all at once, and cook for five minutes, tossing with two forks. Add salt and freshly ground pepper.

3. Remove the skillet from the fire and add the lemon juice.

4. Boil the spaghettini in a large pan of salted water until just *al dente* (see cooking instructions, Chapter 3), drain and transfer to a heated serving dish. Mix the remaining tablespoon of butter into the pasta, pour over the sauce, sprinkle with chopped parsley, mix well and serve immediately, with more salt and a pepper grinder at the table.

LINGUINI CON SPINACI E FUNGHI SECCHI

(Linguini with Spinach and Dried Mushrooms)

Dried mushrooms come mostly in cellophane packages these days. If the package is transparent, check that the slices are large and flat, of a bright color, and with no little insect holes. If you can buy them off the string, or from a jar, sniff to check their perfume. The stronger the perfume, the more aromatic the dish.

This dish calls for fresh spinach with the dried mushrooms, but Swiss chard leaves - without the thick middle stem - can be substituted.

INGREDIENTS:
1 lb. linguini, or any other long thick pasta noodles
1 oz. dried mushrooms, porcini if possible
1 lb. fresh spinach
1/2 cup butter
1/4 cup grated Parmesan cheese
Salt and freshly ground pepper

1. Soak the mushrooms in 1 cup warm water for at least 1/2 hour. Drain, reserving the water, and chop the mushrooms into small pieces.

2. Wash the spinach well, cook it for a few minutes in salted water, and drain. Chop coarsely, and add a tablespoon of the butter. The spinach should still be a bit moist. Add salt and several grindings of pepper.

3. Melt another tablespoon of butter in a small saucepan and add the chopped mushrooms. Strain mushroom water through a cloth, or pour carefully so that sand remains at bottom of the glass, and add to the mushrooms in the pan. Cook for 10 minutes, or until the mushrooms are soft. Set aside.

4. Cook pasta in a large pan of boiling salted water until *al dente* (see cooking instructions, Chapter 3). Meanwhile, melt remaining butter in a large flameproof serving dish. Remove from fire. Drain the linguini, without shaking it dry. Add cooked linguini to the buttered serving dish, and mix well. Add the spinach, then the mushrooms with their liquid, sprinkle over the grated cheese and mix well with two forks. If the pasta seems dry, add a little more butter. Serve immediately, with more cheese and fresh pepper at the table.

MALTAGLIATI AI PISELLI

(Badly-Cut Fresh Pasta with Peas)

A truly indulgent, velvety dish. What makes it fun as well are the Maltagliati, a name which means "badly cut" - a wonderful kind of wide, oddly-shaped fresh pasta that we can simulate using purchased or homemade fresh lasagna strips, sliced into vague triangular shapes of about 1 inch length. Don't be too strict about either the length or the width; they are supposed to look mal-tagliati. This is a rich, sweet beginning to a company meal.

INGREDIENTS:
*1 lb. fresh maltagliati
¹/₂ onion, chopped
2 tablespoons olive oil
1 tablespoon butter
³/₄ lb. fresh peas (shelled weight)
1 teaspoon broth powder
2-3 sprigs fresh tarragon, chopped
1 cup fresh cream
2 egg yolks
¹/₄ cup grated Parmesan cheese
1 small bunch parsley leaves, finely chopped
Salt and freshly ground pepper*

1. Put the chopped onion into a small heavy saucepan, with the olive oil and butter, and cook over a low flame until the onion is completely melted. Add the peas, powdered broth, chopped tarragon and half a cup of water. Cover and cook for 15 minutes, until the peas are completely soft. There should be no more than a tablespoon of water left as broth.

2. With a slotted spoon, transfer half the peas to a food processor and blend well, adding the cream as it purees. Return the puree to the saucepan containing the whole peas, cook for five more minutes, and keep warm while the pasta cooks. Salt to taste and add some freshly ground pepper.

3. Cook the maltagliati in a large pan of boiling salted water until just *al dente* (see cooking instructions, Chapter 3).

4. As the pasta cooks, beat the egg yolks with a fork, add the grated cheese and beat together. Heat the pea puree to boiling point, remove from flame and add the egg-cheese mixture. Mix until cheese is melted.

5. Drain the pasta, transfer to a heated serving dish, pour over the sauce, and mix well so that the pasta shapes are well coated with the sauce. Serve immediately, with some more salt and a pepper grinder at table.

MACCHERONCINI COI PISELLI E PEPERONI

(Macaroni with Peas and Red Peppers)

Another colorful, indulgent pasta. Peas fit so well with buttery cream sauces, that it is really worth waiting for little fresh peas to come along to wallow in these sauces. The juice exuded by the peppers is delicious, and gives the sauce a slightly rosy hue.

INGREDIENTS:
1 lb. maccheroncini, or any other tubular pasta.
3 red bell peppers
4 tablespoons butter
5 oz. fresh sweet peas, shelled weight
1 cup fresh cream
Salt and freshly ground pepper
1/2 cup grated Parmesan cheese

1. Scorch or grill the peppers, skin, remove and discard inner ribs and seeds, and dice into *1/4* inch squares. Set aside.

2. Place the butter and peas in a large saucepan and cook together for several minutes over a low flame. Add the peppers, stirring them into the butter and peas.

3. Add the cream, salt to taste and lots of freshly ground pepper, and cook together over a medium flame until the cream thickens. Remove from heat, to reheat just as the pasta is finishing.

4. Cook the pasta in a generous quantity of salted water until just *al dente* (see cooking instructions, Chapter 3). Drain, transfer to a heated serving dish, pour over the sauce, then half the grated cheese, and mix well. Try to keep the peas integrated throughout the pasta. If you don't succeed, scoop up some peas from the bottom of the dish with each serving. Serve with the remaining cheese at table.

MACCHERONCINI ALL'ORTOLANA

(Maccheroncini with Artichokes and Peas)

Artichokes are another vegetable that go easily into pasta sauces. They must, however, be prepared properly, and that takes a bit of work.

INGREDIENTS:

1 lb. maccheroncini, rigatoni,
  or any other short, tubular pasta
4 small artichokes, or 2 large
2 lemons
1½ lbs. fresh peas (weighed
  with pods), shelled
½ cup butter
½ teaspoon sugar
Salt and freshly ground pepper
⅓ cup fresh cream
⅓ cup grated Parmesan cheese.

1. Prepare the artichokes. Fill a bowl with cold water, squeeze the juice of a lemon into it, and cut a second lemon in half. Remove the tough outer leaves of the artichoke, layer by layer, until you reach the inner, pale green, tender leaves. Slice off the sharp tip of each, and rub the cut part with lemon to prevent discoloration. (Each time you slice the artichoke, rub the cut sides with the second lemon.) Slice the artichoke in half lengthwise (rubbing each half with lemon), and scoop out the fuzzy choke on each side (rubbing each scooped out half with lemon). Turn each half, cut side down, and slice thinly lengthwise, dropping the slices into the acidulated bowl of water. Repeat with all the artichokes.

2. Drain the artichokes and put them into a deep, heavy saucepan, together with the peas, butter and sugar. Add just enough water to cover and cook over a high medium flame, uncovered, for about 20 minutes, or until the water has almost evaporated and the artichokes are tender. (If the peas are not yet soft, add a little more water and cook for another few minutes.)

3. Add salt and freshly ground pepper to taste, the cream, and reheat just to the boiling point. Taste again and add salt.

4. Cook the pasta in a large amount of boiling salted water until just *al dente* (see cooking instructions, Chapter 3). Drain into a heated serving dish, pour over the sauce, sprinkle with the grated cheese, and serve immediately. Mix well at table.

SPAGHETTINI CON CARCIOFI

(Spaghettini with Artichokes)

A most subtle pasta dish - just artichokes melted in butter, a whisper of brandy and lots of cheese.

INGREDIENTS:

1 lb. spaghettini, or any
  other long, thin pasta
6 small artichokes
½ cup butter
1 tablespoon brandy
¾ cup grated Parmesan cheese
Salt and freshly ground pepper

1. Prepare the artichokes as in the recipe for *Maccheroncini all' Ortolana.*

2. Drain from the acidulated water, and place with the butter in a deep heavy skillet. Add just enough water to cover and cook over a lively flame until the water has all but evaporated, about 15 minutes. Add a tablespoon of brandy, salt and a goodly amount of freshly ground pepper.

3. Cook the pasta in a large amount of boiling water until just *al dente* (see cooking instructions, Chapter 3), drain and transfer to a heated serving dish. Pour the artichoke sauce over, add the grated cheese, mix well and serve immediately.

PENNE RIGATE CON ASPARAGI E FAVE

(Ridged Penne with Asparagus and Fava Beans)

Both asparagus and fresh fava beans come onto the market at about the same time in spring. This delicate sauce is a most compatible marriage of the two. To ease the skinning of the inner bean, pour some boiling water over the beans after removing them from their pods; the skin slips right off. The pasta in this recipe is first covered with an asparagus puree, then served in a sauce of beans and asparagus tips.

INGREDIENTS:
1 lb. penne rigate, or any other short pasta
2 lbs. fava beans (about 3/4-1 cup shelled beans)
1 lb. asparagus
1 1/2 cups vegetable broth
2 spring onions, thinly sliced
3 tablespoons olive oil
1 large sprig sage leaves
2 stalks celery, thinly sliced
Salt and pepper to taste
1/3 cup grated Parmesan cheese

1. Remove beans from their pods, blanch with boiling water and remove inner skins. You should have 3/4-1 cup shelled and peeled beans.

2. Wash the asparagus, and slice, reserving the tips. Cook the stems in the vegetable broth for 15 minutes, and remove the asparagus with a slotted spoon, reserving the broth.

3. Slice one of the spring onions and saute in a tablespoon of olive oil. Add the asparagus stems, season with salt and cook for 10 minutes with 1 cup of the reserved broth. Place in food processor and blend to a puree.

4. Chop the remaining spring onions and saute, together with the chopped sage, in remaining 2 tablespoons olive oil. Add the beans and the celery, and cook for 10 minutes. Add some salt and freshly ground pepper, 1/2 cup broth and cook for another 20 minutes, adding more broth if necessary, until the broad beans are cooked. Add the asparagus tips and keep hot.

5. Cook the pasta in lots of boiling salted water until al dente (see cooking instruction, Chapter 3). Drain, transfer to a heated serving dish, and mix in the puree. Mix well, and add the broad bean-asparagus tips sauce. Serve immediately, with grated cheese at the table.

PASTA PRIMAVERA

(Pasta with melange of spring vegetables)

The most elegant, hearty and perfectly sublime of the vegetable pastas. Since Pasta Primavera was invented - not too many years ago, in New York - many variations on the theme have come our way. Different combinations of vegetables, combined with various herbs, sometimes even with a bechamel sauce to bind it - all come under the general definition of "spring pasta", a collection of vegetables gently cooked to a crunchy freshness and served over pasta.

New versions abound, but I still prefer the original given to me by a friend in New York. It is an extravagant pasta. Variations are certainly invited; the only thing I still strongly recommend is NOT to overcook any single vegetable, and to cook each as though it were the main ingredient. The recipe looks much more complicated than it is; it wants time, but you'll find it well worth it.

INGREDIENTS:

1-1½ lbs. spaghetti, spaghettini or other preferred pasta
½ lb. broccoli
3 tiny zucchini
1 lb. fresh green beans
½ lb. fresh (or frozen) peas, (shelled weight)
½ cup olive oil
½ lb. fresh mushrooms, thinly sliced
2 cloves garlic, crushed
2 lbs. fresh ripe tomatoes, skinned, seeded, drained and chopped
1 small hot chili pepper, or ½ teaspoon hot chili relish
¼ cup butter
1 cup fresh cream
½ cup grated Parmesan cheese
2 oz. toasted pine nuts
1 small bunch fresh parsley leaves, chopped
Salt and freshly ground pepper

1. Prepare the vegetables: Separate broccoli flowerets and peel the stems. Slice zucchini lengthwise into quarters, and slice again into 2 inch lengths. Slice green beans lengthwise in half, and again into diagonals about 2 inches long.

2. Each vegetable is cooked separately in the same water. Cook the peeled and sliced broccoli stems for about five minutes in a large amount of boiling salted water. Add the flowerets for the last few minutes of cooking. Remove with slotted spoon to large bowl.

3. Boil the water again, and drop in the zucchini slices. Cook for another five minutes, scoop out with a slotted spoon and add to the bowl of broccoli.

4. Boil up the water and cook the green beans for another five minutes. Drain with a slotted spoon, rinse with cold water to keep them green, and add to the other vegetables.

5. Re-boil the water, add the peas and cook for another five minutes, until just cooked through. Drain and add to the other vegetables. Reserve the cooking water.

6. In a large heavy skillet, heat 2 tablespoons of the olive oil and quickly saute the mushrooms. Add to the other vegetables. Salt the vegetables well, add several good grindings of pepper, and toss. Set aside.

7. Heat the remaining oil and crushed garlic in the same skillet, and add the tomatoes and hot pepper. Cook over a gentle flame for about five minutes, and remove from heat. Pour the entire contents of the skillet into the vegetable, add the chopped basil, and mix.

8. Add more water to the pan in which the vegetables were boiled, enough to cook the pasta. Put to the boil, and add the pasta to cook.

9. While the pasta is cooking, melt the butter in a fire proof casserole large enough to hold the entire dish. Add about ¾ cup (about a ladle full) of the cooking water, then the cream and grated cheese. Heat thoroughly.

10. When the pasta is still very *al dente*, drain it, transfer to the casserole, and mix well with the cream sauce and cheese. Add the vegetable mixture, and toss together over a gentle flame until most of the mixture has been absorbed into the pasta.

11. To serve, sprinkle with the pine nuts and parsley, with more grated cheese and pepper on the table.

PASTAS WITH ROOT VEGETABLES AND DRIED LEGUMES

Less obvious than the vegetable pastas already discussed are those we can make with root vegetables such as onions, leeks, carrots, parsnips, fennel, even kohlrabi and radishes. They can be delicious and are certainly worth trying, especially when you have the ingredients right there.

Here is a small choice to give an idea of what is possible.

MACCHERONI CON CIPOLLE

(Macaroni with Onions)

A deceptively simple dish that incorporates staples usually on hand, with a result that can be served to the most discriminating, even those who pop in at the last minute.

INGREDIENTS:
1 lb. macaroni or any other short, tubular pasta
4 large onions, or 1 leek and 3 onions, all finely chopped
1/2 cup butter
2 eggs
Salt and freshly ground pepper
1/3 cup grated Gruyere cheese

1. Place the chopped onions (or onions and leek) together with the butter in a heavy saucepan with lid. Cover the pan, turn the flame on as low as possible, and cook the onions slowly until they melt into a puree. This will take at least half an hour. Check often to see that enough liquid is retained. If they look at all dry, add some water to keep them moist.

2. Add salt, a good amount of freshly ground pepper and set aside. Up to this stage the dish can be prepared beforehand, and gently reheated before serving.

3. Cook the pasta in lots of boiling salted water until just *al dente* (see cooking instructions, Chapter 3).

4. While the pasta is cooking, beat the eggs well in a large bowl. Remove the hot onion puree from the heat and combine with the eggs. Mix well, making sure all the egg is amalgamated into the onion puree.

5. Drain the pasta, transfer to a heated serving dish, pour over the onion sauce and mix well. Sprinkle with grated cheese and mix again. Serve immediately, with more fresh pepper and grated cheese at the table.

FARFALLE CON CIPOLLE E OLIVE

(Butterfly Pastas with Onions and Black Olives)

Another sweet and simple onion pasta, this time enriched with black olives, and simmered in a full broth.

INGREDIENTS:

1 lb. farfalle, or bow tie pasta
1/4 cup olive oil
2 large onions, thinly sliced (about 1 lb.)
3/4 cup rich vegetable broth
1/2 cup pitted black olives, halved
1 bunch parsley leaves, chopped
1/4 cup grated Parmesan cheese
Salt and freshly ground pepper

1. Put the oil and onions together in a heavy saute pan. Heat over a moderate flame for about five minutes, until the onion begins to soften. Add 1/4 cup of the broth, and cook over a low flame for about 15 minutes, stirring often with a wooden spoon, until the onion is totally melted. Keep the content of the pan liquid, adding more broth if necessary. At the end of 15 minutes, add the remaining broth.

2. Put the pasta to cook in a large pan of boiling salted water until barely *al dente* (see cooking instructions, Chapter 3).

3. While the pasta is cooking, add the black olives, parsley and a good amount of freshly ground pepper to the onions, and continue to simmer over a low flame.

4. When the pasta has just barely cooked, drain it without shaking out the water, and add it to the onion/broth mixture. Mix and stir over a low flame for another five minutes, until the pasta has fully absorbed the broth and is cooked through. Sprinkle in the cheese, and more pepper, mix well and serve, with more cheese and pepper at the table.

PENNE ALLA ROMANA

(Penne with Onions and Ricotta Cheese)

Another recipe that uses a lot of onion, this time elegantly mixed with ricotta and a grated cheese. The chives offset the sweet onion and ricotta with just the slightest bite.

INGREDIENTS:

1 lb. penne, or any other short, tubular pasta
2 large onions, thinly sliced (about 1 lb.)
3 tablespoons olive oil
1/4 cup butter
6 oz. ricotta cheese, broken into small pieces
2 tablespoons grated Parmesan
1 bunch chives, finely chopped
Salt and pepper to taste

1. Put the sliced onions, olive oil and butter in a heavy flameproof casserole, with a lid. Cover, and cook over a low flame for about half an hour, until the onions are completely melted into the oil mixture.

2. After about 1/2 hour of cooking, break up the ricotta into the onions, mix well, and when cheese is just heated - in less than a minute - remove from flame.

3. Cook the pasta in a large amount of boiling water until just *al dente* (see cooking instructions, Chapter 3), drain and transfer to a heated serving dish. Pour the onion sauce over the pasta, add the grated Parmesan, lots of freshly ground pepper and salt. Sprinkle the chopped chives on top, mix well and serve.

CONCHIGLIE CON PORRI, FUNGHI E POMODORO

(Shells with Leeks, Mushrooms and Tomato)

INGREDIENTS:

1 lb. conchiglie (shells) or fusilli
3 leeks, well washed and trimmed
1/4 cup olive oil
3 cloves garlic, pressed
1/2 lb. mushrooms, thinly sliced

4 plum tomatoes, canned or fresh, skinned, seeded and chopped
1/2 cup water
Salt and freshly ground pepper
1 bunch parsley leaves, chopped
1/4 cup grated Parmesan cheese.

1. Wash the leeks well and slice into 1/2 inch sections. Rinse thoroughly to remove any sandy particles. Put the leeks and oil into a deep heavy saucepan, heat over a moderate flame and saute for five minutes. Add the garlic and mushrooms, and saute for three more minutes. Add the tomatoes and water, and continue to simmer. Season with salt and freshly ground pepper.

2. Cook the pasta in a large amount of boiling salted water until just *al dente* (see cooking instructions, Chapter 3). Drain the pasta and transfer to a heated serving dish, sprinkle over the chopped parsley, add the sauce and mix well. Top with the grated cheese, or serve with the cheese separately at table.

MACCHERONCINI ALLE CAROTE

(Little Macaroni with a Carrot Sauce)

This is a recipe that sublimely reveals heights to which the lowly carrot can aspire. One always has carrots on hand. Here is a delicious idea that will yield new respect for you and your carrots. A potato peeler makes slicing the carrots into julienne strips far easier and quicker.

INGREDIENTS:

1 lb. maccheroncini, penne or any other short, fat, tubular pasta
5 small carrots, thinly sliced into long julienne strips
1/4 cup butter
2 tablespoons olive oil
2 tablespoons brandy
1 teaspoon vegetable broth powder

3 tablespoons fresh cream
2 oz. pine nuts, coarsely chopped
1/2 cup grated Parmesan cheese
1 small bunch of parsley leaves, chopped
Salt and freshly ground pepper

1. Put all but a handful of the thinly sliced carrots into a fireproof casserole that can hold the entire pasta. Add half the butter and all of the olive oil, and cook over a low flame for 10 minutes, until the carrots are just cooked through.

2. Add the brandy, increase the flame and allow to evaporate for two minutes. Add the broth powder and the cream, and mix well. Continue to cook over a brisk flame for 5 minutes and remove from heat.

3. Put the pasta into a large pan of boiling salted water to cook until just *al dente* (see cooking instructions, Chapter 3).

4. Drain the pasta and add it to the casserole. Place the remaining butter, the chopped pine nuts and grated cheese on top, and mix well, both from the top and the bottom, mixing in the carrots, their sauce and all the cheese. Sprinkle over the remaining carrots and chopped parsley, add salt and freshly ground pepper, and serve.

SPAGHETTI CON FINOCCHIO

(Spaghetti with Fennel)

Fennel is a most definitive taste, a lovely white bulb with the flavor of licorice. It is difficult to find interesting ways to use it, beyond salad and braising. It smells of the Mediterranean; so many of the local liquors - Pastis, Arak, Raki, Ouzo, Sambuca - have the same anise base. The fields of Provence, of Tuscany, of Greece and Jerusalem abound in the wild version which shares only flavor with the white bulbs that one buys in the shops.

This fennel sauce has a gentle anise flavor that pervades rather than overpowers.

INGREDIENTS:
1 lb. spaghetti
2 fennel bulbs
1 cup fresh cream
2 tablespoons brandy
1/2 cup grated Parmesan
Salt and freshly ground pepper
Fresh olive oil to serve

1. Boil a large pan of salted water in which to cook first the fennel, then the pasta.

2. Clean the fennel bulbs carefully, and cut them into quarters, using only the white bulb and discarding the green parts. Drop the quarters into the boiling water, and cook until just tender. Don't overcook; the texture should remain firm. Remove with a slotted spoon and set aside.

3. Bring the pan of water back to a boil, and drop in the pasta. While the pasta is cooking, squeeze the fennel to rid it of excess water, and slice it into strips about 1 inch wide.

4. In a small saucepan, heat the cream and brandy just to the boiling point. Remove from heat.

5. Cook the pasta until just *al dente* (see cooking instructions, Chapter 3), drain and transfer to a heated serving dish. Mix in the cream and brandy, toss over the grated cheese, a teaspoon of salt and lots of freshly ground pepper. Mix again, and spread the fennel over the top.

6. Mix again at the table, and serve with fresh olive oil and another grinding of pepper.

SPAGHETTI ALLA PANNA CON CIPOLLA

(Spaghetti with Cream and Onion)

The addition of a grated onion to the traditional cream and butter sauce gives a sweet-sharp flavor, whose edge is softened by the cream.

INGREDIENTS:

1 lb. spaghetti, or any other long pasta
1 small onion, grated
1/3 cup butter
1 cup fresh cream
Grated nutmeg to taste
1 small bunch parsley leaves, finely chopped
1/4 cup fresh Parmesan cheese, grated
Salt and freshly ground butter

1. Put the pasta to cook in a large amount of boiling salted water until just *al dente* (see cooking instructions, Chapter 3).

2. Place the grated onion and 3 tablespoons of butter in a small saucepan, and cook over a low flame. When the onion has completely softened, add the cream, about 4 gratings of nutmeg and the finely chopped parsley. Heat just to the boiling point and remove from flame.

3. Drain the cooked pasta, transfer to a heated serving dish, and mix with the remaining butter until the butter has completely melted. Quickly add the cream sauce and mix again. Sprinkle over the cheese, salt and lots of freshly ground pepper and mix thoroughly. Serve, with more pepper at the table.

TAGLIATELLE WITH CREAM AND FRESH HERBS

Fresh herbs are a must here. Use any combination, at least four, and be sure to include tarragon. Select the other herbs according to taste and availability: basil, thyme, parsley, rosemary, marjoram, oregano etc. It's a lush sauce.

INGREDIENTS:

1 lb. fresh tagliatelle or fettuccine
1 small onion, finely chopped
1 clove garlic, pressed
3 tablespoons butter
1 1/2 cups fresh cream
1 large bunch of leaves of mixed fresh herbs, finely chopped
1 tablespoon butter
1/2 cup grated Parmesan cheese
Salt and freshly ground pepper

1. Put the pasta to cook in a large pan of boiling salted water until just barely *al dente* (see cooking instructions, Chapter 3)

2. While pasta is cooking, saute the onion and garlic in the butter. Add the cream, and bring to a boil. Boil for about five minutes, until the cream has somewhat thickened, reduce the flame and add the chopped herbs - tarragon, marjoram, thyme, basil, parsley, oregano. Cook for a few more minutes, and remove from flame.

3. Drain the tagliatelle well and transfer to a heated serving dish. Add another tablespoon of butter, the sauce, a liberal sprinkling of salt and freshly ground pepper, and the grated cheese. Serve with the remaining cheese and more pepper at table.

FUSILLI CON FORMAGGIO, PISTACCHIO E COGNAC

(Corkscrews with Blue Cheese, Pistachios and Cognac)

Blue cheese makes a lovely pasta sauce, especially the Italian sweet Gorgonzola, which is creamier than most and has an almost green vein. If that is unavailable, the Danish Castello is a good substitute. This rich, mild-tasting Gorgonzola-Cognac sauce over little pasta shapes (with the pistachio nuts poking out) is perfect to begin a light dinner of grilled fish - or as a main course in itself. The pound of pasta will serve six to eight as a first course, and four to five as a main course.

INGREDIENTS:
1 lb. fusilli, conchiglini or any other short pasta
3 tablespoons shelled pistachio nuts (about 5 oz., unshelled weight)
2¹/₂ oz. Gorgonzola or other blue cheese
¹/₂ cup butter
2 tablespoons cognac
³/₄ cup fresh cream
Salt and freshly ground pepper to taste

1. Pour some boiling water over the shelled pistachios to help remove the inside skin, and chop coarsely into small pieces.

2. Put the pasta to cook in a large pan of boiling salted water until just *al dente* (see cooking instructions, Chapter 3).

3. While the pasta is cooking, crumble the Gorgonzola into a small saucepan, together with the butter. Melt together over a low fire just until the two are well blended. Add the cream and cook for another minute. Remove from heat, and add the nuts and brandy. Season with salt, and keep warm.

4. Drain the cooked pasta, transfer to a heated serving dish, pour over the sauce, mix well, and serve with pepper at the table.

FARFALLE WITH RICOTTA, BREADCRUMBS AND MARJORAM

This ricotta recipe adds herb-flavored breadcrumbs to a base of ricotta cheese.
Only the breadcrumbs and herbs need a bit of frying in olive oil; otherwise there's no cooking involved.

INGREDIENTS:
1 lb. farfalle, or bowties pasta
1/2 cup olive oil
1/3 cup breadcrumbs
3 sprigs marjoram leaves, chopped
7 oz. ricotta cheese
Salt and freshly ground pepper to taste

1. Put the pasta to cook in a large pot of boiling salted water until just *al dente* (see cooking instructions, Chapter 3).

2. While the pasta is cooking, heat the olive oil in a small pan, and add the breadcrumbs and fry until they are quite crisp, but not burned. Add the marjoram, cook for another minute and remove from flame.

3. Mash the ricotta in a heated serving bowl and add a ladle of the cooking water from the pasta. Add salt and freshly ground pepper to taste, and mix to form a smooth cream.

4. Drain the pasta and add it to the serving bowl with the ricotta. Mix well, pour over the herbed oil, and serve immediately with more pepper at the table.

RIGATONI WITH VODKA, TOMATO AND CREAM SAUCE

The vodka and sharp chili pepper add character to a creamy tomato sauce.

INGREDIENTS:
1 lb. rigatoni, penne, or any other short, tubular pasta
2 tablespoons butter
1 tablespoon olive oil
1 small onion, finely chopped
1/2 lb. fresh ripe cherry tomatoes, halved
1 cup fresh cream
1/4 cup vodka (40 proof)
Pinch of dried sharp chili pepper, to taste.
1/2 cup grated Parmesan cheese
Sprinkling of chopped chives.

1. Combine butter and olive oil in a large, deep skillet, add the chopped onion and saute for about 5 minutes, until the onion is completely transparent.

2. Add the halved tomatoes, and cook gently until the liquid in the pan has almost disappeared, about 1/2 hour. Add the cream, vodka and chili pepper and continue to cook until the sauce is quite thick.

3. Put the penne to boil in a large pot of salted water, and cook until just *al dente* (see cooking instructions, Chapter 3). Drain, transfer to a heated serving dish, pour over the sauce, sprinkle on half the cheese and mix well. Sprinkle with the chopped chives and serve with remaining grated cheese at the table.

FUSILLI WITH SWEETENED COTTAGE CHEESE

This could become a favorite family supper. Children love it.

INGREDIENTS:
1 lb. fusilli (corkscrew pasta)
1 cup cottage cheese
³/4 cup warmed milk
2¹/2 tablespoons sugar
Ground cinnamon to taste
1 tablespoon raisins, or other chopped dried fruit

1. Beat the cottage cheese together with the milk, sugar and cinnamon until smooth. Add the raisins and mix well into the sauce.

2. Cook the fusilli in a large pan of salted water until just *al dente* (see cooking instructions, Chapter 3). Drain, transfer to a heated serving dish, pour over the sauce and serve immediately, while still warm.

GREEN PEPPER RAGÙ

Green peppers make the difference in this ragù , with a distinctive taste that permeates the sauce. Serve it over any of the shorter tubular pastas, such as rigatoni, penne or maccheroncini.

INGREDIENTS:

1/4 cup olive oil
2 medium onions, finely chopped
3 garlic cloves, crushed or finely minced
2 large green peppers, seeded, inner ribs removed, thinly sliced
1/2 lb. chopped lean beef

1 lb. fresh ripe tomatoes (in high season only), skinned, seeded and chopped, or the contents of 1 small can of crushed plum tomatoes
1 cup rich beef stock
Leaves of 3 sprigs marjoram, chopped
Salt and freshly ground pepper to taste

1. Pour the olive oil into a deep heavy casserole and add the chopped onions, garlic and sliced peppers. Saute over a medium-low flame until the peppers are softened, but still firm, about ten minutes.

2. Add the meat, crushing it with a fork to crumble.

3. After a few minutes of cooking, when the meat has just lost its color, add the chopped tomatoes. Mix together, cook for another minute, and pour in the beef stock. Bring to a boil, reduce the flame and simmer for about 45 minutes, uncovered. The sauce should be somewhat thickened. Add the marjoram after about 1/2 hour of cooking, together with salt and freshly ground pepper to taste. This sauce can be made some hours beforehand, and reheated at the last minute.

RAGÙ D'AGNELLO E PEPERONI

(Ragù of Lamb and Peppers)

The Abruzzi region of central Italy, an area filled with shepherds and their sheep, is the home of this recipe. A bit of lamb goes a long way and this pasta dish is as tasty as any lamb dish I can think of.

INGREDIENTS:

2 lbs. fresh ripe tomatoes (only in season) ,or 1 large can of plum tomatoes,
1/2 cup olive oil
3 cloves garlic, crushed or finely chopped
1 lb. lean young lamb, finely cubed
1/2 cup dry white wine

3 red or yellow (or a mixture of both) peppers, seeds and inner ribs removed, thinly sliced
2 bay leaves
Salt and freshly ground pepper
Leaves of about 10 sprigs of parsley, chopped

1. If using fresh tomatoes, skin, drain, remove seeds, chop and set aside. If using canned tomatoes, drain, reserving liquid. Skin, seed and chop tomatoes and set aside.

2. Heat the oil and garlic together in a deep heavy casserole. When the oil around the garlic begins to bubble, add the meat. Brown the lamb on all sides.

3. Add the wine, bring quickly to a boil, and cook for about 5 minutes, or until liquids are reduced to half the original quantity.

4. Add the tomatoes, the sliced peppers and bay leaves, salt and freshly ground pepper, and simmer over a low flame for about 1 1/2 hours, stirring occasionally to make sure that nothing sticks. If the sauce seems too dry, add a little of the reserved tomato juice. After about an hour's cooking, add the parsley. Serve over any pasta, but this one is especially good with the short, tubular pastas.

MACCHERONI ALLA SICILIANA

(Macaroni with Eggplant and Meatballs)

This hearty pasta combines eggplant with tiny meatballs in a rich thick sauce, and works best with any short fat pasta. The pound of pasta should serve five or six people.

INGREDIENTS:

1 lb. short tubular pasta, such as rigatoni or maccheroni
2 large eggplants
4 oz. lean beef, finely chopped
1/2 cup olive oil
1/4 cup flour
2 onions, well chopped
1 bunch parsley leaves, chopped
2 lbs. fresh, ripe tomatoes, skinned, seeded, drained and chopped (see method, Chapter 7), or the contents of 1 large can of crushed plum tomatoes
Salt and freshly ground pepper

1. Peel the eggplants, dice into small cubes, salt liberally and leave to drain in a colander for at least half an hour.

2. Season the beef with salt and pepper, and shape into small 1/2 inch balls.

3. When the eggplant is well drained of its bitter juices, rinse, squeeze out the water and wipe as dry as possible. Heat 1/4 cup of the olive oil in a heavy large saute pan, and fry the eggplant for about ten minutes, until it is soft and golden. Remove with a slotted spoon and allow to drain on paper toweling.

4. Roll the little meat balls in some flour and fry them in the same pan in which the eggplant has cooked, scraping any bits off the bottom and adding a bit more oil if necessary. Remove and set aside.

5. Add the remaining olive oil to the pan, and immediately put in the chopped onions and parsley. When the onions are transparent, add the tomatoes and cook for 15 minutes over a medium flame, allowing the sauce to thicken. Taste for seasoning and add more salt and lots of freshly ground pepper. Add the fried eggplant and meatballs and mix gently.

6. Cook the pasta in a large pan of boiling salted water until *al dente* (see cooking instructions, Chapter 3), drain and transfer to a heated serving dish. Pour the sauce over and mix, trying not to break up the little meat balls.

TAGLIATELLE WITH CHICKEN BREASTS AND ARTICHOKE HEARTS

For a more opulent, richer main course, serve this sauce with fresh green fettuccine noodles.

INGREDIENTS:
1 lb. tagliatelle, or fresh fettuccine
2 chicken breasts, sliced into thin 2 inch long strips
1/2 cup olive oil
1 medium onion, finely chopped
1/2 lb. small champignon mushrooms, wiped clean and thinly sliced
1/2 cup beef stock
6-7 fresh or defrosted frozen artichoke hearts, thinly sliced
The contents of 1 small can of crushed tomatoes
3/4 cup tomato puree (or sauce)
Leaves of 10 sprigs parsley, finely chopped
Leaves of 1 small bunch basil, coarsely chopped
Pinch of sugar

1. In a large heavy skillet, saute the sliced chicken breast in 2 tablespoons of the olive oil just until it has lost its color. Remove the chicken with a slotted spoon and reserve.

2. Add the onion to the pan and cook until it is just transparent. Add the mushrooms and cook gently until they begin to give off their liquid. Add the stock, bring to a boil and immediately add the artichoke hearts. Simmer until the artichokes are tender, about five minutes.

3. Add the tomatoes and the tomato puree, and cook for another 20 minutes, until the sauce has thickened. Add salt and freshly ground pepper to taste, the parsley and basil, and a pinch of sugar if necessary. Taste for seasoning again, and add the chicken. Cook together for another 10 minutes or so while the pasta is cooking.

4. Cook the pasta in a large pan of boiling salted water until just *al dente* (see cooking instructions, Chapter 3). Drain, transfer to a large heated serving dish, pour over the sauce, mix well and serve.

SPAGHETTI DIVERSO

(Spaghetti in Meat and Zucchini Sauce)

This pasta is a fine one-course meal. It combines minced beef, tomatoes, green olives and other good tastes, and needs only a salad and some fruit to complete the meal.

INGREDIENTS:
1 lb. spaghetti
2 lbs. small zucchini
2 medium onions, finely chopped
2 garlic cloves, crushed
1/4 cup olive oil
1/2 lb. lean minced beef
Salt and freshly ground pepper to taste
1 bunch parsley leaves, finely chopped
1 tablespoon dried oregano, or leaves of 4 sprigs fresh.
Contents of 1 small can of crushed tomatoes
4 oz. green olives, pitted and halved, with about 1/4 cup of their juice

1. If zucchini are small, leave unpeeled and slice thinly. If large, peel first, slice lengthwise into quarters and remove seed pods before slicing thinly. Set aside.

2. Place the chopped onion and crushed garlic cloves into a deep heavy saucepan, together with the olive oil, and saute until the onion is transparent, about three minutes.

3. Add the minced beef and brown quickly, only until the meat has lost its pink color.

4. Add the zucchini slices, some salt, the parsley and oregano. Add the tomatoes, mixing them into the other vegetables, and cook slowly, uncovered, for 15 minutes, until the zucchini is cooked through but not mushy. In the last five minutes of cooking, add the olives and their juice.

5. While the sauce is cooking, boil the pasta in a large amount of well salted water until just *al dente* (see cooking instructions, Chapter 3). Drain and transfer to a heated serving dish. Pour over the sauce, add lots of freshly ground pepper, mix well and serve.

PENNE CON FEGATINI

(Penne with Chicken livers)

An inspiration from chopped chicken liver led to the creation of this pasta, which turned out surprisingly well. It has all the makings of good chopped liver, including chicken fat. Not the typical Italian pasta, although chicken fat is definitely a component of the Italian Jewish kitchen.

INGREDIENTS:

1 lb. penne, or any similar, short, tubular pasta
5 oz. chicken livers, prepared
1 small onion, finely chopped
2 heaping tablespoon rendered chicken fat
1/4 cup olive oil
3/4 lb. fresh mushrooms, wiped clean and coarsely chopped
1 lb. fresh ripe tomatoes, skinned, seeded, drained and chopped,
  or the contents of 1 small can of chopped plum tomatoes
1 cup dry red wine
1 small bunch dill, finely chopped
Salt and freshly ground pepper

1. Cut the chicken livers into bite-sized pieces.

2. Put the chopped onion, together with the chicken fat and olive oil into a a deep heavy pan, and cook slowly over a medium flame until the onions are soft.

3. Add the chopped mushrooms, and cook for another 2 minutes, just until mushrooms are well coated with fat. Add the chicken livers and cook over a medium flame for two minutes, until they have lost their red color.

4. Add the tomatoes, salt and several grindings of fresh pepper. When the liquid is bubbling, lower the heat, cover and cook over a low flame for 15 minutes.

5. Meanwhile, put the cup of red wine into a small saucepan and reduce over a high heat to a quarter of its original volume, about 1/4 cup, which will take about 15 minutes. Add the reduced wine to the liver sauce, together with the dill and some more salt.

6. Cook the pasta in a large amount of boiling salted water until just *al dente* (see cooking instructions, chapter 3). Drain, transfer to a heated serving dish, pour over the chicken livers, mix well and serve immediately.

Note: This sauce can be prepared well beforehand and reheated at the last minute, to add to the pasta. Just be sure the livers do not overcook; they get tough.

Spaghettini Con Fegatini, p. 176

PASTA

WITH

FISH

Preserved fish - such as anchovies, tuna, smoked salmon and the like - deserve a special listing in any pasta book. First, there are wonderful ways to use them all in pastas. And more important, we usually have various cans of preserved fish on hand to make up a last minute pasta. Some suggestions follow:

PASTA AND ANCHOVIES

Pasta and anchovies - if you love anchovies - go together beautifully. But there are no two ways with anchovies; one either loves them or hates them. Their taste is distinctive no matter how well camouflaged, whether the little fish are packed in oil, or bought out of large cans, where they are preserved in salt. I always prefer to buy the salted anchovies when I see them. When rinsed and filleted, they seem firmer than the oil-preserved sort. Once opened, anchovies must be used as soon as possible. I find myself tempted to throw in the whole lot even when only a few are called for in a single recipe. They have a tendency to go saltier and saltier, and take on a much stronger taste once they remain open to the air for any length of time.

Anchovies preserved in salt are packed in large cans, sold by weight, and need a bit more care than those packed in oil. They must be cleaned under running water (never soaked), and filleted. This is quite easy; just chop off head and tail and split them open with a paring knife (imported Portuguese anchovies are especially firm and tasty.) If using salted anchovies to make the recipes below, substitute 4 or 5 filleted anchovies for each can mentioned in the ingredients list.

For a milder anchovy taste, there is the anchovy paste one buys in tubes. It also lasts longer than any other, and can be used in whatever quantities you like. Use it as a milder substitute in any of the recipes below. All of these recipes have anchovies as a main ingredient; other recipes that include anchovies can be found elsewhere (see index).

SPAGHETTI CON ACCIUGHE E UOVA

(Spaghetti with Anchovies and Egg)

This anchovy sauce is a rich, creamy and pleasant dish that must be eaten just as soon as it reaches the table in its hot serving dish. For a milder flavor, use fewer anchovies. For anchovy lovers, it is a treat.

INGREDIENTS:

1 lb. spaghetti
4 oz. Gruyere cheese
2 whole eggs
1 2-oz. can anchovies, drained and chopped, or 4 salted anchovies, rinsed, filleted and chopped

3 tablespoons butter
Salt and freshly ground pepper

1. Grate the cheese coarsely and set aside in a cool place.

2. In a food processor, blend the eggs and the chopped anchovies. Gradually add the grated cheese, blending all the time, to ensure that the cheese works evenly into the mixture. The final mixture should be a creamy paste.

3. Put the pasta to boil in a large amount of salted water. While the pasta is cooking, melt the butter in a large flameproof serving dish that can hold the finished pasta. Add $1/2$ cup of the water in which the pasta is cooking, and keep warm over a low flame.

4. Drain the pasta just before it becomes *al dente*. It should still be somewhat hard to the bite. Add it to the butter dish, and mix well, continually, for a few minutes until all the butter-water has been amalgamated and the pasta is *al dente*.

5. Add the anchovy-cheese mix, remove from flame and continue to mix the pasta until it becomes perfectly creamy. (Don't cook the egg sauce; you'll end up with scrambled eggs.) Serve immediately, with lots of freshly ground pepper at the table.

MACCHERONI ALLE ACCIUGHE CON POMODORO

(Macaroni with Anchovies and Tomatoes)

A very Neapolitan dish, sharp and spicy, the perfect complement to anchovies.

INGREDIENTS:

1 lb. macaroni, or any other short, tubular pasta
$1/2$ cup olive oil
3 cloves garlic, crushed
1 2-oz. can anchovies, drained and chopped, or 4 salted anchovies, rinsed, filleted and chopped

1 large can of crushed tomatoes.
1 bunch parsley leaves, chopped well
Freshly ground pepper

1. Heat the olive oil and pressed garlic together in a heavy skillet, over a medium flame. When the oil around the garlic begins to bubble, add the anchovies. Mash the anchovies with a fork as they begin to cook, until they dissolve.

2. Add the tomatoes, and cook for ten minutes. Add the chopped parsley, and some good grindings of pepper, lower the flame, and continue cooking while the pasta is cooking.

3. Cook the pasta in a large amount of boiling salted water until just *al dente* (see cooking instructions, Chapter 3). Drain and put half the noodles on the bottom of a flameproof casserole, equipped with a lid. Pour over half the sauce, then spread again the remaining noodles and sauce, cover and cook for three minutes over a low flame. Serve immediately.

ACCIUGHE CON AGLIO E FORMAGGIO

(Anchovy Sauce with Garlic and Cheese)

An anchovy sauce that calls for the paste, but canned or salted anchovies may be used instead.

INGREDIENTS:

1 lb. spaghettini, or any other long, thin pasta
3 tablespoons butter
1/4 cup olive oil
2 cloves garlic, crushed
1 1/2 tablespoons anchovy paste
1 bunch parsley leaves, finely chopped
1/4 cup Parmesan cheese
Freshly ground pepper, and salt, if necessary

1. Place the butter, the olive oil and crushed garlic into a heavy skillet over a medium heat. When the oil around the garlic begins to bubble, remove from heat.

2. Add the anchovy paste and half the chopped parsley. Mix well, return to stove and cook over a low flame while the pasta is cooking.

3. Cook the pasta in a large pan of boiling salted water until just *al dente* (see cooking instructions, Chapter 3). Drain, transfer to a heated serving dish, pour over the anchovy sauce and mix well. Sprinkle the remaining parsley on top, along with the grated Parmesan, and mix well again. Serve immediately, with lots of freshly ground pepper at the table.

FUSILLI CON ACCIUGHE ED OLIVE NERE

(Fusilli with Anchovies and Black Olives)

A Sicilian dish, with a sharp Mediterranean flavor.

INGREDIENTS:

1 lb. fusilli, or any other short pasta
2 cloves garlic, pressed
1/2 cup olive oil
1 2-oz. can anchovies, drained and chopped, or 4 salted anchovies, rinsed, filleted and chopped
4 oz. black olives, stoned and chopped
1 lemon rind, grated
1 bunch parsley leaves, finely chopped
1/2 hot little pepper, or 1/2 tsp. hot chili relish
1/4 cup grated Parmesan cheese
Freshly ground pepper, and salt, if necessary

1. Put the olive oil and crushed garlic into a deep, heavy skillet over a medium flame. When the oil around the garlic begins to bubble, add the anchovies. Mash with a fork, over a medium flame, until the anchovies dissolve.

2. Add the olives, lemon rind, parsley and hot pepper and cook for another minute. Reduce the flame, and keep warm while the pasta is cooking. Add half a ladle of the cooking water to the sauce.

3. Cook the pasta in a large pan of boiling salted water until just *al dente* (see cooking instructions, Chapter 3). Drain, add the pasta to the skillet containing the sauce and cook for a minute, mixing all the while. Pour into a heated serving dish, sprinkle over the grated cheese, mix well and serve with a pepper grinder at the table.

SPAGHETTI CON BURRO E ACCIUGHE

(Spaghetti with Butter and Anchovy Paste)

An easy sauce with anchovy paste.

INGREDIENTS:
1 lb. spaghetti
¹/₂ cup butter
3 tablespoons anchovy paste
White pepper

1. Melt the butter in a small pan and add the anchovy paste. Cook just until the paste has melted into the butter.

2. Cook the pasta in a large amount of boiling salted water until just *al dente* (see cooking instructions, Chapter 3), drain (saving some of the cooking water) and transfer pasta into a heated serving dish. Pour over the sauce, adding two tablespoons or more of the cooking water to keep it from sticking. Season with white pepper when served.

SPAGHETTINI AROMATICI

(Spaghetti with Anchovies, Capers and Basil)

A further elaboration on the lush taste of the Mediterranean. This one combines fruity olive oil, basil, anchovies, black olives, garlic and capers. Any leftover sauce can be soaked up with fresh bread. The sauce can be prepared while the pasta is cooking; just have all the ingredients ready beforehand. A satisfying meal.

INGREDIENTS:
1 lb. spaghettini, or any other long, thin pasta
4 oz. pitted black olives, chopped
1 small bunch basil leaves, coarsely torn
2 tablespoons capers, rinsed and coarsely chopped
²/₃ cup fresh, fruity olive oil
3 garlic cloves, pressed
1 2-oz. can anchovies, drained and chopped, or 4 salted anchovies, rinsed, filleted and chopped
Freshly ground black pepper, and salt if necessary
1 small bunch parsley leaves, finely chopped

1. Mix the olives, basil and capers together in a small bowl. Set aside.

2. Start the pasta cooking in a large pan of boiling salted water.

3. Put the oil and garlic together in a heavy skillet, over a medium flame. When the oil around the garlic begins to bubble, add the chopped anchovies. Mash the anchovies with a fork until they dissolve into the oil.

4. When the spaghettini is cooked just *al dente* (see cooking instructions, Chapter 3), drain and transfer to a heated serving dish. Sprinkle over the olive and caper mix and pour over the anchovy oil. Mix thoroughly, taste for salt and add lots of freshly ground pepper. Mix again and serve immediately.

PASTA AND TUNA FISH

I find tuna preserved in water best for pasta sauces. Most of the recipes below call for olive oil in addition; one can drain the water and use a fresh olive oil. If you do use oil-packed tuna, it is advisable to drain the oil and replace it with olive oil for the recipes below.

Most of us usually have a can of tuna in the cupboard, and it can serve splendidly for an unexpected meal. Tuna can also have a surprising effect when used in a pasta sauce. Most of the pasta recipes below call for handy ingredients; they are for that moment when there is "nothing" in the house to eat, and you need a quick interesting meal. Ingredients can be substituted one for another with interesting results: Green olives instead of black, anchovies instead of capers, tomato sauce for canned tomatoes. Just remember to remember that tuna can always make a pasta sauce.

SPAGHETTI CON TONNO [1]

(Spaghetti with Tuna Fish [1])

A natural mix of tuna and tomatoes. The capers add a nice piquancy, but can be omitted if not available.

INGREDIENTS:
1 lb. spaghetti
¹/4 cup olive oil
3 cloves garlic, chopped
2 lbs. fresh, ripe tomatoes, skinned, drained and seeded,
  or the contents of 1 large can of crushed tomatoes
1 bunch parsley leaves, finely chopped
1 small hot pepper, or ¹/2 tsp. hot chili pepper (optional)
1 can tuna fish, preferably packed in water, drained
1 tablespoon capers, chopped
Salt and freshly ground pepper

1. Put the olive oil and chopped garlic together in a deep heavy skillet, and heat over a medium flame until the oil around the garlic begins to bubble.

2. Add the tomatoes, parsley and chili pepper, and cook over a moderate flame until mixture becomes a thick puree, about 20 minutes. Add the drained tuna and capers. Mix well, taste for salt, and add freshly ground pepper as well. Keep warm while the pasta is cooking.

3. Cook the pasta in a large amount of boiling salted water until just *al dente* (see cooking instructions, Chapter 3). Drain, transfer to a heated serving dish, pour over the sauce and mix well before serving.

SPAGHETTI CON TONNO [2]

(Spaghetti with Tuna Fish [2])

This pasta combines tuna, tomatoes and anchovies, with both olive oil and butter. It's a rich, mildly piquant taste.

INGREDIENTS:

1 lb. spaghetti
2 tablespoons butter
1 2-oz. can anchovies, drained (about 8 fillets)
1 can tuna, drained
2 garlic cloves, pressed
1/3 cup olive oil

1 lb. fresh ripe tomatoes, skinned, seeded and chopped, or the contents of 1 small can of crushed plum tomatoes
1 bunch parsley leaves, finely chopped
Salt, if needed, and freshly ground pepper

1. Allow the butter to soften to room temperature. When soft, mash together with the anchovies to make a paste.

2. Put all but one tablespoon of olive oil into a deep heavy saucepan, together with the crushed garlic. Heat over a moderate flame, and when the oil around the garlic begins to bubble, add the tomatoes and some grindings of pepper. Cook for about 15 minutes, reduce the flame and keep warm.

3. In a separate, smaller saucepan, heat the remaining tablespoon of olive oil and add the tuna. Break the tuna up and fry for a minute. Add the tuna to the tomato sauce, and mix well.

4. Cook the spaghetti in a large pan of boiling salted water until just *al dente* (see cooking instructions, Chapter 3). Drain, transfer to a heated serving dish, and add the anchovy butter. Mix until pasta is well coated with the anchovy, then pour over the tomato sauce, sprinkle on the parsley, mix well and serve immediately.

SPAGHETTI CON TONNO [3]

(Spaghetti with Tuna Fish [3])

This pasta has the odd mixture of fish and cheese, a combination that would raise the eyebrows of any proper Italian.

INGREDIENTS:

1 lb. spaghetti
1 can tuna fish, preferably packed in water, drained
3 fillets anchovies, drained and chopped
10 black olives, stoned and chopped
1/2 cup olive oil

1 lb. fresh ripe tomatoes, skinned, drained, seeded and chopped, or the contents of 1 small can of crushed plum tomatoes
4 oz. Bel Paese cheese, diced
Salt and freshly ground pepper

1. In a mortar, or food processor, blend the tuna, anchovies, and olives together until well amalgamated. Add a little olive oil, or the water from the tuna, to make mixture more workable and give it the consistency of a thick paste. Remove the paste to a small saucepan and heat over a low flame just to the boiling point, no further. Remove from flame.

2. In another pan, heat the remaining olive oil and add the tomatoes. Cook for 15 minutes, and meanwhile cook the pasta.

3. Cook the pasta in a large amount of boiling salted water, until just *al dente* (see cooking instructions, Chapter 3). Drain and transfer to a heated serving dish. Immediately add the diced cheese and mix well.

4. Add the tomato sauce, and the anchovy-tuna paste, and mix into the cheese-coated pasta. Serve with a generous sprinkling of freshly ground pepper and salt, if necessary.

SPAGHETTINI CON TONNO E PISELLI

(Spaghettini with Tuna and Peas)

Another natural combination, using canned and frozen produce usually on hand.

INGREDIENTS:
1 lb. spaghettini, or any other long, thin noodle
4 oz. frozen peas
2 tablespoons butter
1/3 cup olive oil
1 clove garlic, pressed
1 7-oz. can tomato sauce
1 can tuna fish, drained
1 small bunch parsley, finely chopped
Salt and freshly ground pepper to taste

1. Cook the frozen peas together with the butter and a pinch of salt over a low fire, until the peas are thoroughly defrosted, about five minutes. Keep warm.

2. Put the pasta to cook in a large pan of boiling water until just *al dente* (see cooking instructions, Chapter 3).

3. Put the olive oil and pressed garlic into a deep heavy saucepan, and heat over a medium flame. When the oil around the garlic begins to bubble, add the tomato sauce, the pea-butter mixture, and the tuna, broken up into small pieces. Heat through and cook over a low flame for two or three minutes.

4. Drain the pasta, transfer to a heated serving dish, pour over the sauce, add a generous sprinkling of chopped parsley, salt and freshly ground pepper to taste, and serve immediately.

PENNE CON TONNO E FUNGHI FRESCHI

(Penne with Tuna and Fresh Mushrooms)

A sauce that is made in two parts and separately added to the pasta, first tomatoes, then mushrooms. The mushrooms, served over the dressed pasta, retain their distinct consistency.

INGREDIENTS:

1 lb. penne, or any other short, tubular pasta
$1/2$ cup olive oil
2 cloves garlic, separately crushed
1 2-oz. can anchovies, drained, chopped and divided in two
2 lbs. fresh ripe tomatoes, skinned, seeded, drained and chopped, or the contents of 1 large can of crushed plum tomatoes
1 can tuna fish, preferably packed in water, drained
1 heaping tablespoon oregano, rubbed through the palms
1 teaspoon unsalted butter, softened to room temperature
$1/2$ lb. fresh mushrooms, thinly sliced
1 small bunch parsley leaves, finely chopped
Salt and freshly ground pepper

1. Put $1/4$ cup olive oil and 1 pressed garlic clove into a deep heavy saucepan, over a moderate flame. When the oil around the garlic begins to bubble, add $1/2$ of the chopped anchovy fillets and mash into the oil with a fork. Add the tomatoes, and cook for fifteen minutes over a low flame.

2. Add the tuna fish, and cook for another few minutes. Taste for salt, add freshly ground pepper and the oregano. Keep warm.

3. Mash together the remaining anchovies with the softened butter into a paste.

4. Pour the remaining olive oil - $1/4$ cup - into a skillet with the second pressed garlic clove, and heat over a moderate flame. When the oil around the garlic begins to bubble, add the sliced mushrooms and saute for just two minutes, long enough to cook the mushrooms without their becoming soft. Add the mashed anchovy-butter, mix well and remove from flame.

5. Cook the pasta in a large amount of boiling salted water until just *al dente* (see cooking instructions, Chapter 3), drain and transfer to a large, heated serving dish.

6. Mix the tomato sauce well with the pasta, and top with the mushrooms, without mixing. Sprinkle over some chopped parsley and serve immediately.

PASTA WITH FRESH AND FROZEN FISH

Both fresh and frozen fillets of fish work well with pasta, and can often serve instead of shellfish to make a rich and satisfying seafood pasta. The recipes in this section are a few suggestions what one can do with both fresh and frozen fish. The trick with frozen fish is to make utterly sure it does not overcook. Fresh fish with pasta is, of course, a real treat. The recipes here call for grouper or bass, sweet and delicate fish, but other sweet, full-fleshed fish can be also used.

LINGUINI CON CERNIA

(Linguini with Grouper)

It's possible to prepare this sauce some hours before cooking the pasta. Store covered in the refrigerator, and just heat through before mixing with the pasta.

INGREDIENTS:
1 lb. linguini
3 cloves garlic, pressed
1 bunch parsley leaves, finely chopped
1/2 cup freshest olive oil
1 lb. grouper, filleted
1/2 cup dry white wine
1 1/2 cups tomato sauce
Salt and freshly ground peppe

1. Chop the garlic and parsley together very finely, and divide in two. Saute half the quantity in the olive oil just until the oil begins to bubble around the garlic.

2. Add the fish fillets and cook for a minute. Season with salt and pepper and pour over the wine. Allow the wine to bubble up for another minute, and using a slotted spoon, remove the fish from the sauce to a plate. Set aside.

3. Add the tomato sauce to the pan and cook over a lively flame for about ten minutes, until the sauce is somewhat thickened. Add salt and pepper and return the fish to the pan. After five minutes, break the fish into small pieces with a fork, add the remaining parsley-garlic mix and remove from fire.

4. Cook the pasta in a large pan of boiling salted water, drain into a heated serving dish and pour over the sauce. Add salt if needed, lots of freshly ground pepper, mix gently but thoroughly and serve.

LINGUINI MARINARA ALLA TOSCANA

(Linguini with a Tuscan Fish Sauce)

Frozen fish fillet is recommended for this sauce only for economy's sake, as a nutritious and economical meal. If a full-fleshed fresh sea fish is available, however, it is definitely recommended. While similar to the previous sauce, this one takes on a sharp piquant taste, a very Tuscan quality. Most fish sauces along the Tuscan coast in Italy bury a little hot chili pepper somewhere in the full mixture of tomato and fish. This recipe is ample enough to stretch to 1½ or even 2 lbs. of pasta.

INGREDIENTS:
1 lb. linguini, or any other long pasta.
1 lb. filleted fish defrosted
3/4 cup olive oil
1 medium onion, finely chopped
4 cloves garlic, pressed
1/2 cup white wine
1 lb. fresh ripe tomatoes, skinned, seeded and chopped, or the contents of 1 small can of crushed plum tomatoes
1 can tomato concentrate
1/2 cup warm water.
1 small piece chili pepper, or 1/2-1 teaspoon hot chili relish
1 heaping tablespoon oregano
1 bunch parsley leaves, finely chopped
Salt and freshly ground pepper

1. Put the defrosted fish fillet together with 1/4 cup olive oil and 2 tablespoons of water into a shallow pan, large enough to hold the fillet in one layer (in one or two pieces). Cook over a low flame until the fillet is just cooked through. Remove from flame, and set aside.

2. Put the remaining 1/2 cup olive oil, the onion and the garlic into a large heavy pan or casserole, and saute until the onion is golden. Add the wine, turn up the flame and simmer for three minutes.

3. Add the tomatoes, dilute the tomato concentrate with the water and add to pan, together with the hot chili pepper. Remove the fish from its liquid to a plate, and pour the liquid into the sauce. Bring to a boil and cook rapidly for 15 minutes, stirring frequently.

4. Taste for seasoning, add salt and lots of freshly ground pepper, and more hot pepper if desired. Rub in the oregano and cook for another few minutes.

5. Add the fish fillet, broken into bite-sized pieces, and the parsley, and keep warm while the linguini is boiling - do not allow fish to cook.

6. Cook the linguini in a large pan of boiling salted water until just *al dente* (see cooking instructions, Chapter 3). Drain, transfer to a heated serving dish, pour over the sauce, mix well and serve.

SPAGHETTINI AI FRUTTI DI MARE FINTI

(Spaghettini with Mock Seafood Sauce)

A taste of the sea, albeit a bit contrived. Canned tuna is hardly frutta di mare. *But the results are surprisingly seafood-like, and a lot less expensive. Fake shrimp and crabmeat-like sticks can even be added for a more "authentic" feel. It's all very deceptive. (The sauce can be made earlier, and reheated only to boiling point when the pasta is ready; make sure not to overcook it; the fish fillet must remain firm and juicy.)*

INGREDIENTS:
1 lb. spaghettini, or any other long, thin pasta
1 frozen fish fillet (preferably haddock or other firm, juicy fish)
1 cup dry white wine
1/2 large can white breast of tuna (preferably packed in water)
1 can anchovy fillets, drained of their oil, finely chopped
1 tablespoon softened butter
1/2 cup olive oil
1 small onion, finely chopped
4 cloves garlic, pressed
1 lb. fresh ripe tomatoes, skinned, seeded and finely chopped,
  or the contents of 1 small can of crushed plum tomatoes
3 sprigs fresh marjoram, or 1 heaping tablespoon oregano
1 short sprig rosemary leaves, finely chopped
1 small chili pepper, or 1/2 teaspoon hot chili relish
1 small bunch parsley leaves, finely chopped
Salt and freshly ground pepper

1. Cook the fish fillet - frozen or just thawed - in 1/2 cup white wine over a medium flame until it has just lost its transparency. Drain, reserving the cooking liquid, and break the fish into small, bite-sized pieces.

2. Mash chopped anchovies together with butter, to make a paste. Set aside.

3. Put the oil, garlic and onion in a deep saucepan or casserole, and saute over a medium flame until the oil begins to bubble around the garlic. Add the mashed anchovies, and mash into the oil with a fork, until anchovies dissolve into the oil.

4. As soon as the anchovies are melted, add the remaining 1/2 cup wine. Boil for a minute or two over a high flame.

5. Reduce the flame, and add the tomatoes, the marjoram, rosemary and hot chili pepper, the tuna and liquid in which the fish fillet was cooked. Cook for five minutes and taste for seasoning. Add lots of freshly ground pepper, salt if necessary and the chopped parsley.

6. Cook the spaghettini in a large pan of boiling salted water until just *al dente* (see cooking instructions, Chapter 3), drain and transfer to a heated serving dish. Pour over the sauce, mix well and serve immediately.

PASTA AND SALMON

These are truly party pastas, rich, creamy and delicate. They afford an elegance that stretches a little smoked salmon into a meal for six people (see Salad section for a summer pasta with smoked salmon).

SPAGHETTI WITH TWO SALMON SAUCE

This combination of both smoked and fresh (or frozen) salmon makes for an elegant and sublime party dish.

INGREDIENTS:
1 lb. fresh tagliatelle or fettuccine, or spaghetti
³/4 cup dry white wine
¹/2 cup vegetable stock (or fish broth, if possible)
1¹/2 cups fresh cream
1 lb. fresh salmon, skinned and sliced into about 12 pieces
¹/2 cup fresh or frozen peas
2 oz. smoked salmon, cut into matchstick pieces
2 tablespoons grated Parmesan
Leaves of 1 small bunch parsley, chopped

1. Put the tagliatelle to cook in a large pan of boiling salted water just until *al dente* (See cooking instructions, Chapter 3).

2. As you put the water to boil, begin the sauce. In a large flat skillet, boil the wine, the stock and cream until mixture is slightly reduced and thickens, about 10 minutes.

3. Add the salmon fillet pieces and the peas, and cook just until the salmon is cooked through, about 8 minutes. Stir in the smoked salmon and simmer gently for a minute or two, until the sauce has thickened still more.

4. Drain the pasta, and put it into the simmering sauce. Mix gently until all the cream is absorbed, pour into a heated serving dish, and top with the grated cheese and parsley. Mix again at the table.

FARFALLE CON CAVIALE E VODKA

(Farfalle with Caviar and Vodka)

Another very refined pasta, worth splurging on for a special occasion. Red salmon caviar is the right one for this dish. The tangy taste of vodka and lemon marry perfectly with the fat juicy little lumps; it is a refreshing pasta and quite beautiful to look at.

INGREDIENTS:
1 lb. farfalle
3 spring onions,
1 lemon, both rind and juice
2 tablespoons butter
1/2 cup vodka
1 large jar of fat salmon caviar (About 3 1/2 oz.)
3 tablespoons olive oil
Salt and freshly ground pepper to taste

1. Chop spring onions finely, with as much of the green part as is fresh. Cut lemon rind into very thin strips and set aside.

2. Put the spring onions and butter into a large casserole, and cook slowly over a low flame. When the onions are tender, turn up the flame and throw in the vodka.

3. Allow the vodka to evaporate and add the thinly sliced lemon rind. Let cook a minute and turn off the flame. Add the caviar, and gently work it into the sauce. Add pepper.

4. Cook the farfalle, drain and transfer to the preheated casserole. Pour the lemon juice over the pasta, and mix well. Add the olive oil and mix again. Finally, spread the vodka-caviar sauce across the top and serve, making sure that each portion receives a fair amount of caviar.

BAKED PASTAS

CHAPTER THIRTEEN

The *pasticcio* is the most practical of pasta dishes, the single sort that can be almost fully finished well before it's needed at the table. There are simple *pasticcios* and elegant *pasticcios,* and they can range from an eggplant/penne mix to a crusty timbale, a pastry shell filled with fresh pasta.

Pasticcio is a wonderful Italian word that basically means a confusion, or a mess. (*Bel pasticcio!* It's a fine mess!) Given over to pasta, it stands for one that's been thrown together with any number of ingredients, bound with tomato sauce or bechamel and cheese, and baked in the oven to finish off crisply.

Lasagne, being well ordered and arranged, are not really *pasticcios.* *Timballi* could be called *pasticcios,* but, generally, as crust-embellished pasta-pies, they are much too elegant to be addressed in the vernacular. There's also a recipe here for a pasta torte, which is a really unusual way for Italians to serve pastas; it's much more Greek. The Greeks also call their pasted-together oven-baked macaroni a *pasticcio.*

The single, and most important, quality that *lasagne, pasticcios, rotoli* and *timballi* have in common is the fact that they all go into the oven for a second cooking. Most can serve as a one-course meal, or an elegant buffet addition, or even as a first course in an otherwise light meal.

The *lasagne* calls for a wide flat noodle, usually a fresh egg pasta. It can be green or white, either purchased or home made (see Chapter 5, on homemade pastas). *Lasagne* can usually be assembled some hours before serving, but they should never be baked earlier to be reheated for guests (or anyone else). Save the cooking until the last minute.

Pasticcios usually require one of the shorter pastas, a simple tubular shape like the penne, or a more intricate one, like fusilli or large shells. The thicker pastas have a role here; they maintain their shape better when cooked twice, as the recipe requires. And, for a buffet casserole, they can be eaten without the aid of a knife. Don't assemble *pasticcios* beforehand. The sauce can be prepared and kept warm, the pasta cooked. Mix them, however, at the last moment before popping the casserole into the oven. When mixed beforehand, the pasta continues to absorb the liquid, and you will end up with an overcooked, overdry, real "mess".

The *rotolo* and *timballo* are showpieces of the pasta world, dishes that take time and patience. The rewards are ample. The rotolo is a large sheet of pasta, which is filled, rolled, baked with a sauce in the oven and sliced at the table. In a *timballo,* a rich crust serves as the container for a freshly-made tagliatelle or gnocchi bathed in a rich and colorful sauce, topped by a crisp layer of cheese and baked in the oven for a golden finish.

LASAGNE DI MAGRO

(Meatless Lasagne)

A lasagne that makes good use of eggplant, and adds some tuna, mozzarella, black olives and capers for a nourishing supper dish.

INGREDIENTS:
1 lb. fresh lasagne noodles
2 large eggplants
Light oil for frying
2 lbs. fresh tomatoes, skinned, seeded and sliced into long strips, or the contents of 1 large can of whole tomatoes, drained and sliced into strips
1 good bunch basil, chopped
Contents of 1 can tuna, drained
1/2 lb. mozzarella, cut into small cubes
1 1/2 cups grated Parmesan cheese
5 oz. black olives, pitted and halved
2 tablespoon capers
3 sprigs fresh oregano
Butter
Salt and pepper

1. Slice the eggplants lengthwise, then into long strips about the length of a finger, much like for French frying potatoes. Place in a colander, salt liberally and allow to drain for about an hour.

2. Cook the lasagne strips, a few at a time, in a large pan of boiling salted water, until just *al dente*, and remove to a pan of cold water.

3. Dry the eggplant strips and deep fry them in a light oil until golden. Allow to drain on paper toweling.

4. Place all other ingredients in small bowls and place within easy reach,

5. Butter liberally a large rectangular baking pan and line with a layer of lasagne leaves. Distribute over the pasta half of the tuna, half of the fried eggplant strips, a third of both cubed cheeses, a third of the black olives, tomato strips and the chopped basil.

6. Cover with a second layer of pasta, spread it with remaining tuna and eggplant, another third of the cheeses, black olives, tomato and basil.

7. Add a third layer of pasta, and over that distribute the remaining cheese, olives, tomatoes and basil. Add the capers and the chopped oregano. Drizzle generously with olive oil, add salt and place in a 350 degree oven for about *1/2* hour, until it is all bubbly and golden. Serve hot.

GOAT CHEESE AND SUN-DRIED TOMATO LASAGNE

Sun dried tomatoes and a mild goat cheese combine in this modern application of traditional Italian products. It's surprisingly good. The fresh lasagne leaves need not be cooked before assembling the lasagne - the very liquid sauce will cook them in the oven.

INGREDIENTS:
1 scant lb. fresh lasagne noodles (see Chapter 5)

BECHAMEL:
1/4 cup unsalted butter
1 large onion, finely chopped
2 garlic cloves, minced
1/2 cup all-purpose flour
1 cup vegetable broth
1 cup fresh cream
1 1/2 cups milk

FILLING:
3/4 lb. mildly salted goat cheese, crumbled (Feta does nicely here)
Salt and freshly ground pepper
1/2 nutmeg, grated
1/2 lb. ricotta cheese
1/4 cup sun-dried tomatoes, preferably oil packed, drained of their liquid and chopped
1/4 cup grated Parmesan cheese

1. To make bechamel, melt the butter in a heavy large saucepan over medium-low heat. Add the chopped onion and garlic and cook until translucent, about 10 minutes.

2. Add the flour and stir into a non-lumpy paste. Whisk the vegetable broth in slowly, and cook for about 5 minutes, stirring constantly, until very thick. Add the cream and milk and continue to stir often until the sauce has gently thickened, about 30 minutes. Stir in goat cheese, and season, if needed, with salt. Add lots of freshly ground pepper and the nutmeg.

3. Butter the bottom of a large rectangular baking dish. Spread a few tablespoons of the bechamel/goat cheese sauce across the bottom, and place over a quarter of the lasagne leaves, slightly overlapping. Sprinkle half of the broken-up ricotta cheese over the pasta, and cover with another quarter of the lasagne noodles.

4. On this layer of the noodles, spread half of the bechamel/goat cheese sauce, and sprinkle over half of the sun-dried tomatoes. Place another quarter of the lasagne leaves on top, and then, the remaining ricotta cheese.

5. Place the final layer of lasagne leaves, and cover with remaining sauce and sun-dried tomatoes. Sprinkle the grated cheese across the top. Up to this stage the lasagne can be prepared as much as a day in advance. Cover and refrigerate, and bring to room temperature before continuing. The actual cooking must be done at the last minute.

6. Preheat the oven to 350 degrees. Bake the lasagne until crisp and bubbling, about 20 minutes. Allow to rest for a few minutes before serving.

LASAGNE VERDI

(Green Lasagne)

Lasagne Verdi, made with fresh green (spinach) lasagne noodles, is the traditional Bolognese pasta dish. It is made of a rich combination of ragù and bechamel. This recipe fits a deep oven-proof rectangular pan, but lasagne noodles can be cut to fit an oval or round casserole as well.

It is not easy to gauge the amounts exactly, so it is probably better to have more than you need. Leftover pasta sheets can always be frozen; if there is not enough for another lasagne, the pasta leaves can be cut into odd shapes and served as maltagliati (see index.)

Always bake the lasagne at the last minute, and leave it to rest for about 10 minutes before serving. Leftovers can be reheated or served at room temperature.

INGREDIENTS:
1 scant lb. fresh green lasagne egg pasta (see Chapter 5)
Ragù recipe (see Chapter 11)

BECHAMEL:
5 oz. margarine
1/2 cup all-purpose flour
4 cups hot beef broth
1/2 nutmeg, ground
Dried oregano
Salt and freshly ground pepper
Paprika

1. Prepare the ragù, as described in Chapter 7.

2. While the ragù is cooking, prepare the bechamel. Melt the margarine in a large saucepan. Sprinkle in the flour and work into a smooth paste, cooking until the flour browns slightly into a golden color. Gradually pour in the hot, well flavored meat broth, stirring all the time to prevent lumps forming. Grind in the nutmeg, add salt to taste and several grindings of pepper.

3. Reduce the flame and simmer the sauce, stirring frequently, for about five minutes. It should have the consistency of thick cream. If it is too thick to spread easily, dilute with a little broth or water. If it is too thin to hold its shape when spread across the pasta, cook a while longer to thicken.

4. Bring a large pan of water to the boil, with a heaping tablespoon of salt. Lower to a simmer, and cook the pasta leaves, a few at a time, just long enough to become pliable. Remove with a slotted spoon and plunge immediately into a bowl of cold water, to keep them from sticking to one another. Lay on a dry cloth. Continue until all the pasta has been gently cooked.

5. To assemble lasagne, place all ingredients within easy reach. Skim a bit of ragù from the top and spread it over the bottom of the lasagne pan.

6. Line the bottom of the pan with a layer of pasta, just barely overlapping each pasta sheet with the next, so that the pasta covers the bottom completely while not crawling up the sides. On this spread a thin layer of ragù, covering the entire surface.

7. Spread a thin layer of bechamel over the ragù, and sprinkle the bechamel with some dried oregano. Cover the bechamel with another layer of pasta, and then another layer of ragù, another layer of bechamel and oregano. Repeat the process for two more layers, ending with a layer of ragù. Cover with a last layer of pasta, and spread with remaining bechamel and oregano.

8. Sprinkle paprika liberally over the top of the bechamel. Up to this stage, the lasagne can be prepared well before time. Leave the baking, however, until the last minute.

9. Preheat the oven to 375 degrees, and bake the lasagne for about 20 minutes, until the top layer is a rich golden color and the sauce is bubbling around it. Allow to rest for several minutes before serving.

MUSHROOM-TOMATO LASAGNE

Lots of mushrooms, lots of tomato sauce and bechamel make this a wonderful first dish for a festive occasion. The abundant amount of liquid will suffice to cook the pasta in the oven, so there is no need to pre-cook the lasagne leaves.

INGREDIENTS:

1 scant lb. fresh lasagne pasta
1 oz. dried porcini mushrooms
1 1/4 lb. bright fresh mushrooms
1/3 cup olive oil
2 garlic cloves, crushed
1 medium bunch parsley leaves, finely chopped

Salt and freshly ground pepper
1 large can of crushed tomatoes, or 2 lbs. of fresh tomatoes, skinned, drained, seeded and coarsely chopped
5 sprigs fresh oregano leaves, chopped, or 2 tablespoons dried

BECHAMEL:

1/4 cup butter
3 tablespoons flour
4 cups milk
1/4 nutmeg, grated
3/4-1 cup grated Parmesan cheese

1. Soak the dried mushrooms in a cup of warm water for at least 20 minutes. Gently remove them from the water, making sure to leave the sand behind, and chop finely. Reserve soaking water.

2. Wiped fresh mushrooms clean; if bruised, peel. Slice thinly, with as much stem as possible.

3. Heat the oil and garlic together in a large saute pan that will hold all the mushrooms and the tomatoes. When the garlic turns golden, add the chopped porcini mushrooms, and carefully pour in about 1/2 cup of their soaking water (be sure to leave the sand behind). Cook over a high flame until the water has completely evaporated.

4. Add the fresh mushrooms and chopped parsley and continue to cook for another minute. Add the tomatoes, salt and lots of freshly ground pepper, and the oregano. Mix, cook one more minute and remove from flame.

5. Prepare the bechamel. Melt the butter in a large saucepan, add the flour and mix well into a paste. Add the milk slowly, whisking all the time, and bring to a slow boil. Add the nutmeg, and mix to a thin creamy consistency.

6. To assemble the lasagne, place all the ingredients, the mushroom/tomato sauce, the bechamel, and the cheeses, within easy reach. Grease the bottom of a large baking pan, and spread a very thin layer of bechamel across. Place a layer of pasta on top, covering the bottom of the pan. Now spread a layer of tomato/mushroom sauce across the pasta, then a layer of bechamel, and then a good sprinkling of grated Parmesan cheese.

7. Repeat for two or more layers, using up all of the tomato/mushroom sauce, but not the bechamel or cheese. Spread the remaining bechamel over the last layer of pasta, sprinkle liberally with cheese. Up to this stage, the lasagne can be prepared some hours before baking.

8. Heat the oven to a hot 400 degrees, and bake the lasagne for 10 to 15 minutes, or until the top is golden brown and bubbling. Allow to rest for five minutes before serving.

LASAGNE DI FUNGHI E FORMAGGIO

(Mushroom and Cheese Lasagne)

This delicate lasagne is really a combination of lasagne leaves and sliced mushroom, without the usual tomato or bechamel. Although rich, it's fairly light and makes a lovely first course for a company dinner

INGREDIENTS:
1 lb. fresh lasagne leaves
1 1/4 lbs. firm young white mushrooms
2 cloves garlic, sliced
3/4 cup butter
2 teaspoons lemon juice
Salt and freshly ground pepper
4 1/2 oz. mozzarella, cubed
1/4 cup grated Parmesan cheese
1/4 cup ricotta cheese
1 cup fresh cream

1. Wipe the mushrooms clean, and slice thinly, with stems. Saute the mushrooms with the garlic in 1/4 cup of butter, just until the mushrooms begin to melt, about five minutes. Add the lemon juice, salt and lots of freshly ground pepper. Set aside.

2. Preheat the oven to 350 degrees, and butter a large shallow attractive baking pan.

3. Cook the lasagne leaves in a large pan of simmering salted water, a few leaves at a time, until just *al dente*. Drain with a slotted spoon or wooden handle, and drop into a pan of cold water. Lay out the pieces on a dry cloth.

4. Cover the bottom of the buttered baking dish with a quarter of the lasagne noodles, and over the lasagne spread a third of the cubed mozzarella. On top of the cheese, spread a third of the mushrooms with some of the juice. Dot with a quarter of the remaining butter, and sprinkle over a quarter of the grated cheese.

5. Repeat the process three times more, ending with the fourth layer of lasagne. Dot with the remaining butter and sprinkle over the remaining Parmesan.

6. Blend the ricotta into the fresh cream, and pour the mixture over the top of the lasagne. Add salt and grind some pepper across the top. Cover with foil and bake in the preheated oven for 20 minutes. Remove foil and bake, uncovered, for another 10 minutes before serving.

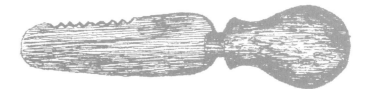

LASAGNE ALLE VERDURE

(Vegetable Lasagne)

A dish filled with goodness and color - orange carrots, green peas and red tomatoes. Other vegetables can be substituted if the suggested ones are not available. Use similar amounts.

INGREDIENTS:

1 scant lb. fresh lasagne leaves (see Chapter 5)
1 lb. fresh young carrots, sliced into thin matchsticks of about 1½ inches
1 lb. fresh peas (shelled weight) or 1 package frozen
1 lb. fresh ripe tomatoes, skinned, seeded and finely chopped,
  or the contents of one small can of crushed plum tomatoes
¼ cup butter
⅓ cup olive oil
2 cloves garlic, pressed
1 tablespoon flour
1½ cups milk
½ cup grated Parmesan, plus 2 tablespoons for topping
1 bunch basil leaves, coarsely chopped
Salt and freshly ground pepper

1. In a large pan of simmering salted water, cook the pasta, a few strips at a time. Plunge into cold water, and lay on a towel until ready to use. Repeat until all pasta is cooked.

2. Cook the carrot sticks in salted water, in a saucepan large enough to hold the peas as well. When the carrots are just tender, add the peas and cook for five more minutes. Drain, and place in a bowl together with the chopped tomatoes. Set aside.

3. Heat the butter and oil, and add the chopped garlic. When the butter has stopped bubbling, add the flour. Mix into a paste, stir in the milk and cook just long enough for the sauce to thicken slightly. Remove from flame. Add the grated Parmesan, the chopped basil, salt and lots of freshly ground pepper. Mix well, making sure the cheese is evenly amalgamated into the sauce. If the sauce becomes lumpy, reheat over a low flame, stirring, just until the cheese is melted.

4. To assemble the lasagne, place all ingredients around a rectangle or round baking dish. Oil the bottom of the dish, and cover with a layer of pasta strips, overlapping them slightly but not allowing them to creep up the sides. Spread a sparse layer of vegetables over the pasta, and top with 2 or 3 tablespoons of cheese sauce.

5. Cover with a second layer of pasta, then another sparse layer of vegetables and sauce. Continue the process until all the vegetables are used up, but save enough cheese sauce to cover a final layer of noodles. Sprinkle with the remaining grated cheese. Up to this point the lasagne can be prepared in advance, and put into the oven just before serving.

6. To serve, heat the oven to 350 degrees, and bake the lasagne for about 20 minutes, until the top is golden and bubbling. Allow to rest for five minutes before serving.

LASAGNE DI CARCIOFI

(Artichoke Lasagne)

The lemon juice gives this lasagne a slightly tangy flavor that adds an interesting taste. The pasta will cook with the milk in the oven; if very fresh, there is no need to pre-cook it.

INGREDIENTS:
1 scant lb. fresh green lasagne leaves.
8-10 artichokes
2 lemons
1/4 cup butter
1 cup grated Parmesan cheese
1/4 cup mozzarella (1 ball), finely chopped
Salt and freshly ground pepper

BECHAMEL:
1/4 cup butter
3 tablespoons flour
4 cups milk
Salt and freshly ground pepper.

1. Prepare the artichokes: Snap off the outer leaves right down to the most tender light green middle leaves. Slice off 1 1/2 inches from the top. Quarter the artichoke, rubbing each exposed side with half a lemon to prevent discoloration, and, with a sharp paring knife, slice out all the fuzz. Slice each quarter lengthwise, as thinly as possible, and drop immediately into a bowl of water acidulated with the juice of 1 whole lemon.

2. When all the artichokes have been prepared in this manner, drain and put them into a large flat saute pan. Add water just to cover, and 1/4 cup of butter. Cook over a medium-high flame until all the water has evaporated, and the artichokes are tender. They should be perfectly cooked when the water has gone. Salt well and transfer to a large bowl.

3. Prepare the bechamel - melt butter in a large saucepan, add the flour and mix into a paste. Slowly add the milk, whisking all the time, to make a sauce the consistency of thick cream. Season with salt to taste, and lots of freshly ground pepper.

4. Mix three quarters of the bechamel sauce into the artichokes, reserving the remaining quarter for the top layer of lasagne. Mix the two cheeses in another bowl.

5. To assemble the lasagne, arrange all ingredients within easy reach. Liberally butter the bottom of a large baking dish, and line with sheets of pasta. Spread over the pasta a thin layer of the artichokes with bechamel, and sprinkle liberally with the cheeses.

6. Add another layer of pasta, and again a layer of artichokes and cheese. Repeat for two more layers, using up the entire artichoke mixture, but not the cheese. End with a layer of pasta.

7. On the last layer of pasta, spread the remaining bechamel sauce, and sprinkle the remaining cheese on top. Add some more salt, and grind some pepper across the top. Up to this stage the lasagne can be prepared some hours before serving.

8. Preheat the oven to 400 degrees, and bake for 15-20 minutes, until a golden-brown crust has formed. Allow to rest a bit before serving.

CANNELLONI

Cannelloni are filled and rolled squares of pasta that can easily be made from wide fresh lasagne leaves. The pasta is rolled out thinly, and cut into squares 4-5 inches in size, then gently filled, folded from both sides, laid in a baking pan and lightly covered in sauce, for the final baking. The following two recipes give an idea of what a cannelloni can be. Any of the fillings for the stuffed fresh pastas in Chapter 5 can also be used for filling cannelloni. Two important caveats: Do not over-fill the pasta; the filling should be a complement, not a large gluey glob. The same rule goes for the sauce; a light sauce should complement the filled pasta, not drown it.

CANNELLONI ALLA NAPOLETANA

(Neapolitan Cannelloni)

This deceptively simple-sounding dish takes a bit of practice to assemble in just the right way, but its virtual melt-in-the-mouth quality makes it well worth the effort. This recipe, like the one following, serves eight to ten amply for a main course, and more at a buffet.

INGREDIENTS:

1 scant lb. of wide lasagne leaves, cut into 4 inch lengths
$^1/_2$ cup olive oil
2 large cans of chopped tomatoes, or 4 lbs. fresh, ripe tomatoes, skinned, seeded, drained and chopped
1 teaspoon vegetable broth powder
$^1/_2$ cup boiling water
1 bunch parsley leaves, chopped
1 bunch basil leaves, finely chopped
1 can anchovies, drained and finely chopped
$^1/_2$ cup grated Parmesan cheese
$1^1/_2$ cups ($10^1/_2$ oz.) mozzarella cheese, coarsely chopped

1. Prepare the filling. Heat the olive oil in a large heavy pan, and add the chopped tomato pulp. Season with salt and pepper, and cook over a medium flame for 15 minutes.

2. Divide the tomatoes in half, in two bowls. Dissolve vegetable broth in the boiling water, and add to one half of tomato mixture, together with parsley and basil. Mix and set aside.

3. Place the chopped anchovies and chopped mozzarella in two separate bowls.

4. In a large pan of simmering salted water, cook the pasta squares a few at a time (not more than four), for no more than a few minutes, until they are just *al dente*. Remove from pan one at a time, most easily accomplished over the handle of a long wooden spoon. Drop them in a bowl of cold water.

5. To assemble the cannelloni, oil a large baking dish that will hold all the cannelloni in one layer. Take the pasta squares from the cold water one at a time, and lay on a dry cloth. On each square, spread a teaspoon of the plain chopped tomato, and cover with a teaspoon of chopped mozzarella, a bit of the anchovy and a sprinkling of the grated Parmesan. Fold from both sides, turn over and place in the baking dish. Repeat, snugly nestling the cannelloni side by side in the baking dish, until all the ingredients - except for the grated Parmesan - are used up.

6. Spread the blended tomato and stock mixture across the top, and sprinkle over the remaining Parmesan. Up to this stage, the dish can be prepared well ahead of time.

7. Preheat the oven to 350 degrees, and bake the cannelloni for twenty minutes, until the top is bubbling.

CANNELLONI CON FUNGHI

(Mushroom-filled Cannelloni)

This recipe, will will serve 10 as a main course, and more as part of a buffet.

INGREDIENTS:
1 scant lb. of wide lasagne leaves, cut into 4 inch lengths
1¼ lbs. mushrooms
1 medium onion, finely chopped
¼ cup olive oil
¼ cup butter
¼ cup light goat cheese, crumbled

BECHAMEL:
¼ cup butter
2 tablespoons flour
2 cups hot milk
½ cup grated Parmesan cheese
Salt and freshly ground pepper
½ teaspoon nutmeg

1. Wipe mushrooms clean, peel them if bruised, and chop coarsely, with stems. Set aside.

2. To make filling, melt the butter in the oil and add the chopped onion. Saute until the onion becomes transparent, and add the chopped mushrooms. Cook only until the mushrooms begin to water, about 5 minutes. Set aside. When the mushrooms have cooled, add the crumbled goat cheese, salt if needed and lots of freshly ground pepper.

3. Cook the pasta squares in a pan of simmering salted water, a few at a time, just until *al dente*. Remove with a slotted spoon and drop into another pan of cold water.

4. Butter a large baking dish that will hold all the cannelloni in a single layer. Take one square at a time, lay it on a dry cloth, place a tablespoon of filling along the middle, and fold the two sides over. Turn and arrange, folded side down, in the baking dish. Tuck in all of the cannelloni snugly, side by side.

5. To make the bechamel topping, melt the butter, stir in the flour and slowly add the hot milk, whisking all the time. Season with salt, half the grated Parmesan, nutmeg and lots of freshly ground pepper, and cook for fifteen minutes over a low flame, stirring often.

6. Spread the bechamel over the cannelloni, and sprinkle the remaining grated Parmesan over the top. Up to this stage the cannelloni can be prepared some hours before serving.

7. Preheat the oven to 350 degrees, and bake the cannelloni for 30 minutes until the top is golden and bubbly.

PASTICCIOS

There are a few things to remember when preparing a pasticcio. The pasta should not be cooked for too long in its first boiling, before being combined with other ingredients. At its best it should still be somewhat al dente *when brought from the oven. Nor, for the same reason, should the pasticcio be assembled before the last minute. Pasta has a tendency to continue to absorb liquid and will bloat with all the sauce, only to dry during the second baking. It should also be noted that 1 lb. of pasta goes further in most casseroles than in a normal pasta.*

Pasticcios can be made with just about every fresh vegetable. Especially suited are vegetables that add color to the pasta, and go well with a particular pasta sauce or bechamel. For main courses, a ragù or sauce with pieces of chicken can be combined with vegetables and a short pasta, baked to crisp the top and handsomely served.

PASTA FRESCA CON MELANZANE

(Fresh Pasta Leaves and Eggplant)

Fresh lasagne leaves (see Chapter 5) are used in this dish, although it is not exactly a lasagne, nor cannelloni. The lasagne rather forms a crusty-edged basket for sauteed eggplant, tomato sauce and mozzarella cheese, all baked together to a wonderful melange. The pasta is not cooked first.

INGREDIENTS:

Fresh lasagne made with 2¹/₂ cups flour and 3 eggs (see Chapter 5)
1¹/₄ lbs. eggplant
1 large can of crushed tomatoes or 2 lbs. fresh ripe tomatoes, skinned, seeded, and finely chopped
3 cloves garlic
2 sprigs basil leaves, finely chopped
4 sprigs fresh oregano leaves, finely chopped
1 small hot chili pepper, chopped, or a pinch of chili powder
¹/₂ cup olive oil
Salt
Flour
Oil for frying
1 lb. fresh mozzarella cheese

1. Slice the eggplant, with its skin, into 1/4 inch rounds, and place on a colander or plate. Salt liberally and allow to sweat while you prepare the remaining ingredients.

2. Place the chopped tomatoes in a bowl. Add the pressed garlic, the chopped basil, 1/2 of the oregano, the chili pepper, olive oil and salt to taste. Marinate for about an hour.

3. Dry the eggplant slices gently, dust them with flour and fry in a small amount of oil, preferably olive oil. Allow to drain on paper towels.

4. Preheat the oven to 375 degrees. Oil a large baking dish, and spread a very thin layer of chopped tomatoes (with some marinade) across the bottom. Over this place the lasagne strips, overlapping them slightly one on the other, and overlapping the edge of the baking dish by about 2 inches.

5. Slice the mozzarella into 1/4 inch rounds. Fill the baking dish with alternating layers of eggplant, mozzarella and tomatoes. Add a sprinkle of chopped oregano to each layer.

6. Just before reaching the final layer, fold in the edges of the pasta, forming a closed package. Apply the final layer of eggplant, mozzarella, tomatoes and oregano on top, and bake in the pre-heated oven for 45 minutes.

PASTICCIO DI MELANZANE

(Eggplant Pasticcio)

Like most popular pasticcios, this is a simple eggplant casserole that really serves any occasion: a buffet, a family supper, even a children's party. If you don't finish it in one sitting, it reheats wonderfully the next day. The following amount serves six amply as a main course, and as part of a buffet will serve ten or more.

INGREDIENTS:
1 lb. penne, cartwheels, fusilli, shells or other short pasta.
2 large eggplants
Oil (preferable light olive) for frying (as little as possible)
3 cloves garlic, 1 whole, 2 pressed
3 tablespoons olive oil
1 1/2 cups tomato sauce, or the contents of 1 large can of crushed tomatoes
1/4 cup butter
1 small bunch fresh basil leaves, chopped
1 small bunch fresh parsley leaves, chopped
1/2 cup grated Parmesan cheese

1. Cut the unpeeled eggplant into 1 inch cubes, salt liberally and rest in a colander for at least half an hour to allow the bitter juices to drain. Squeeze out as much water as possible before beginning to fry.

2. Heat the frying oil in a large saute pan with the whole garlic clove, and remove the garlic when it browns. Fry the eggplant cubes, a small amount at a time, just until they are browned, and dry on kitchen toweling.

3. Wipe dry the saute pan and put in 3 tablespoons of olive oil with the 2 remaining pressed garlic cloves. When the oil around the garlic begins to bubble, add the tomato sauce or crushed tomatoes, as well as several grindings of pepper, and cook over a high flame for about five minutes. Reduce the flame, and simmer while the pasta cooks.

4. Cook the pasta in a large amount of boiling salted water until just barely *al dente* (see cooking instructions, Chapter 3). Drain and pour into a large bowl. Mix in the butter, and then the tomato sauce, chopped herbs and half the grated cheese. Add the eggplant and mix again well. Taste for seasoning, add salt and lots more pepper.

5. Preheat the oven to a high 400 degrees. Pour the pasticcio into a large attractive baking dish, and bake for 15 minutes. Sprinkle over the remaining cheese and serve.

Note: The eggplant and tomato sauce can be prepared well beforehand. But cook the pasta and do the mixing less than an hour before you plan to bake and serve.

SPAGHETTINI AL FORNO CON POMODORO

(Spaghettini and Fresh Tomato Pasticcio)

A deliciously simple and fresh tasting pasticcio. Here the tomatoes must be at their ripest to gain the full taste of the finished dish.

INGREDIENTS:
1 lb. spaghettini
1½ lbs. freshest, ripest tomatoes, skinned, but left whole
2 garlic cloves, finely chopped
1 small bunch parsley leaves, finely chopped
2 tablespoons dried oregano, or leaves of 6 sprigs fresh
1 cup freshest virgin olive oil
4 tablespoons fresh breadcrumbs, made from day old bread
Salt and freshly ground pepper

1. Scald the tomatoes with boiling water and remove skins. Slice them rather thickly, and divide them into three piles.

2. Mix and chop together the garlic, parsley and oregano, and set aside.

3. Cook the spaghettini in a large pan of boiling salted water until not quite *al dente* (see cooking instructions, Chapter 3).

4. While the pasta is cooking, oil the bottom of a large casserole, big enough to hold the entire pasticcio. Sprinkle a thin layer of breadcrumbs (half the total) over the oil, and on top arrange a third of the tomato slices in one layer. Sprinkle with some of the garlic/parsley/oregano mixture, salt liberally and grind pepper all over the top.

5. Drain the pasta without shaking out all the water, and return it to its cooking pot. Pour over ³/4 cup of the oil, and mix it well into the spaghettini, making sure the pasta is well coated. Spread about half the pasta over the bottom layer of tomatoes.

6. Put another third of the tomatoes over the pasta, and again sprinkle on more of the garlic/parsley/oregano mixture, some more salt and lots of pepper. Spread the remaining pasta over the tomato slices, and pour over any remaining oil in the pan.

7. Preheat the oven to 400 degrees. Mix the remaining breadcrumbs with the remaining garlic/parsley/oregano mixture. Place the final third of the tomato slices on top, and sprinkle the breadcrumb mixture over. Salt and pepper liberally, and dribble over the remaining olive oil. Bake, uncovered, for 20 minutes.

TEGLIA SAPORITA

(Penne on Fresh Tomatoes)

Another dish of fresh tomato slices, this time baked with aromatic herbs and olives that give the pasta a special flavor.

INGREDIENTS:
1 lb. ribbed penne, or any other short, tubular, ribbed pasta
7 tablespoons olive oil
1¹/₂ lbs. fresh tomatoes, sliced
2 cloves garlic
1 bunch basil leaves, chopped
2 sprigs oregano leaves, chopped

1 small piece chili pepper
5 oz. olives (black, green or both), pitted and sliced (about 1¹/₂ cups)
1/4 cup grated Parmesan cheese
2 tablespoons breadcrumbs
Salt and freshly ground pepper

1. Heat the oven to 400 degrees. Grease a large baking dish with 1 tablespoon olive oil.

2. Slice the tomatoes fairly thickly, and place them in one layer on the bottom of the baking dish.

3. Chop one clove garlic, mix with the basil and oregano leaves and sprinkle over the tomatoes. Salt well, add a dripping of 2 tablespoons olive oil, and bake in the preheated oven for fifteen minutes.

4. Put the pasta to boil in a large pan of salted water until just *al dente* (see cooking instructions, Chapter 3).

5. Drain the pasta into a large terrine. Press remaining garlic clove into a large saute pan with 4 tablespoons olive oil, the chili pepper and sliced olives. Cook for a few minutes and pour the sauce over the pasta. Mix well, add salt and lots of freshly ground pepper, and spread the pasta over the tomatoes in the baking dish.

6. Sprinkle the grated cheese atop the pasta, then the breadcrumbs, and drip the remaining oil across the top. Put in the hot oven for another seven minutes to crisp the top, and serve immediately.

PASTICCIO DI CONCHIGLIE CON CIPOLLE, POMODORO E FORMAGGIO

(Onion, Tomato and Cheese Pasticcio)

Lots of onions and cheese, with an addition of tomato, are what's special here. It's mostly a sweet sauteed onion taste.

INGREDIENTS:
1 lb. large conchiglie (pasta shells) or any other short pasta
2/3 cup butter
1/2 cup olive oil
2 garlic cloves, crushed
2 medium onions, thinly sliced
1 small can tomato concentrate
1 small can of crushed plum tomatoes, or 1 lb. fresh ripe tomatoes, skinned, seeded, drained and chopped
5 sprigs fresh oregano, chopped, or 1 tablespoon dried.
1/2 lb. mozzarella, cubed
1/2 cup grated Parmesan cheese
Salt and freshly ground pepper

1. Put *1/3* cup of the butter in a heavy saute pan, together with the oil, crushed garlic and sliced onions, and cook slowly over a medium flame until the onions are well melted, about 20 minutes.

2. Add the tomato concentrate and crushed tomatoes, and cook over a lively flame for another 15 minutes. Add salt, lots of freshly ground pepper and the oregano. Keep simmering while the pasta cooks.

3. Cook the pasta in a large pan of boiling salted water until barely *al dente* (see cooking instructions, Chapter 3). Drain, transfer to a large mixing bowl, and immediately add the remaining butter and the mozzarella and mix thoroughly.

4. Preheat the oven to 350 degrees. Put the shells into a deep baking dish, scraping in any cheese and butter remaining in the mixing bowl. Pour over the tomato sauce, mix again gently (leaving most of the sauce on top), sprinkle over the grated cheese, and bake, uncovered, for 15 to 20 minutes, until the pasticcio bubbles.

PASTICCIO DI PENNE RIGATE CON PEPERONI

(Penne with Red Peppers Pasticcio)

A soothing pasticcio, a combin–ation of grilled red peppers and bechamel sauce, poured over ridged penne and baked in the oven until golden.

INGREDIENTS:
10 oz. penne, rigate or any other short pasta
2 large red peppers

BECHAMEL:
2 tablespoons butter
2 tablespoons all-purpose flour
2 cups milk
3 tablespoons tomato concentrate
Leaves of 5 sprigs basil, chopped

1 small bunch parsley leaves, chopped
2 cloves garlic, pressed
$^2/_3$ cups grated Parmesan cheese

1. Roast the peppers over a flame or under a grill until they are blackened, skin, remove seeds and inner ribs, and cut into thin strips.

2. To make the bechamel, melt the butter in a small casserole, add the flour, mix well and gradually add the milk, mixing steadily until sauce thickens. Add salt and lots of freshly ground pepper. Cook for about 10 minutes, and add the tomato concentrate.

3. Add the chopped basil and parsley to the sauce together with the pressed garlic cloves. Finally add the peppers. Mix well and keep warm.

4. Preheat the oven to 425 degrees. Cook the penne in a large pan of boiling salted water until *al dente*, drain, and mix with the pepper sauce. Pour into an oiled baking dish, top with the grated cheese and bake for about 15 minutes, until bubbly.

PASTICCIO DI MACCHERONCINI, POMODORO E FORMAGGIO

(Tomato and Cheese Pasticcio)

An enticing mix of bread crumbs and oregano adds a special flavor to an otherwise straightforward tomato/mozzarella oven pasta.

INGREDIENTS:

1 lb. short, rounded little maccheroncini, or any other short pasta
3/4 cup olive oil
2 lbs. fresh ripe tomatoes, skinned, seeded, drained and chopped, or the contents of 1 large can of plum tomatoes, drained, seeded and chopped
2 cloves garlic, crushed
Leaves of 5 sprigs oregano, finely chopped, or 2 tablespoons dried oregano
3/4 cup day-old white bread, crumbled without crusts.
1 bunch parsley, finely chopped
5 oz. mozzarella, diced into small cubes
1/2 cup grated Parmesan cheese
Salt and freshly ground pepper

1. Put 1/2 a cup of the olive oil, the tomatoes, garlic and half of the oregano into a deep saucepan, and cook over a medium flame for 10 minutes. Season with a teaspoon of salt and some good grindings of pepper, and remove from flame.

2. Mix the crumbled bread with the parsley and remaining oregano, rubbing them together to a rough mixture.

3. Cook the pasta in a large amount of boiling salted water until just barely *al dente* (see cooking instructions, Chapter 3). Drain.

4. Oil a large attractive baking dish, and spread a third of the pasta across the bottom. Cover with a third of the tomato sauce, a third of the mozzarella, a third of the grated cheese and finally, with a third of the breadcrumb/herb mixture. Dribble a third of the remaining olive oil over the top. Season with some salt and grindings of pepper.

5. Repeat the procedure twice, at the final layer reversing the order of grated cheese and breadcrumb/herb mixture. End with a layer of grated cheese and a dripping of olive oil on top.

6. Preheat the oven to 350 degrees. Cover the baking dish with foil and bake for 20 minutes. Remove foil and bake, uncovered, for another 10 minutes, or until the top is golden and the pasta bubbling.

CONCHIGLIE RIPIENE

(Stuffed Shells)

The shells in this pasticcio are not really stuffed, but should be firm and so well mixed that each shell comes out filled with sauce.

INGREDIENTS:

10 oz. large conchiglie (large pasta shells)
2 slices white bread
1/4 cup milk
1 cup cottage cheese
2 eggs, beaten
1 bunch parsley, finely chopped
Leaves of 5 sprigs basil, finely chopped
1/4 nutmeg, grated, or 1/4 teaspoon ground nutmeg
1/3 cup grated cheddar or sharp Parmesan cheese
1 large can of crushed plum tomatoes
1/4 cup butter
Salt and freshly ground pepper

1. Remove crust from bread slices, soak in milk and squeeze dry. Set aside.

2. Cook the pasta shells in a large amount of boiling salted water until they are just *al dente* (see cooking instructions, Chapter 3). Preheat oven to 350 degrees.

3. While the shells are cooking, mix together the cottage cheese, eggs, soaked bread, parsley and basil. Add salt to taste, the nutmeg, half the grated cheese and mix well.

4. Drain the shells into a large mixing bowl, add the sauce and turn round and round until each shell is well filled with sauce. Spread into a buttered baking dish.

5. Pour the crushed tomatoes over the entire surface of the shells. Dot with butter, sprinkle over the remaining grated cheese, and bake for 30 minutes.

PASTICCIO DI ACCIUGHE E FUNGHI

(Anchovy and Mushroom Pasticcio)

The taste of anchovies, not overwhelming, definitely distinguishes the flavor of this dinner dish.

INGREDIENTS:
1 lb. large conchiglie, or any other short pasta
1 lb. fresh mushrooms, wiped clean and coarsely chopped
3/4 cup olive oil
3 garlic cloves, pressed
1 can anchovies, drained and chopped
1 bunch parsley leaves, finely chopped
3 tablespoons fresh breadcrumbs
Salt and freshly ground pepper

1. Place the mushrooms, 2 tablespoons of olive oil and a tablespoon of water in a deep saute pan. Sprinkle liberally with salt and cook over a lively flame for five minutes. Remove the contents to a large bowl.

2. Wipe the same pan dry. Put all but 1 tablespoon of the remaining olive oil into the pan, together with the garlic and chopped anchovies. Cook over a medium flame, mashing the anchovies into the oil and garlic. When the anchovies have almost disappeared, remove from flame and add the contents to the mushrooms. Add chopped parsley and mix well.

3. Cook the pasta in a large pan of boiling salted water until barely *al dente* (see cooking instructions, Chapter 3). Drain and mix well with the mushrooms.

4. Preheat the oven to 425 degrees. In a small saucepan, heat the remaining tablespoon of oil. Add the breadcrumbs and cook together for a minute. Remove from flame.

5. Oil a large baking dish, and pour in the pasta, scraping in any remaining oil from the bottom of the bowl. Top with the fried breadcrumbs and bake for seven or eight minutes.

PASTICCIO DI FETTUCCINE

(Fettuccine Casserole)

A rich and delicate tasting casserole of fresh egg pasta, cheese and eggs. If you prefer a sharper taste, use a sharper cheese.

The perfect dish to use for this recipe is a deep baking casserole that is flameproof as well. If such a dish is not handy, make the preparations in a deep heavy saucepan and transfer the entire pasticcio to a baking dish for the final baking.

INGREDIENTS:

12 oz. fresh fettuccine
3 eggs, separated
1/2 cup butter
2 tablespoons flour
2 1/2 cups milk
1/2 cup grated Parmesan
1/2 teaspoon ground nutmeg
Salt and freshly ground pepper

1. Separate the eggs, and beat the whites until they form soft peaks.

2. To prepare a bechamel, melt 1/3 cup butter in the baking dish or a heavy saucepan, add the flour and mix to form a paste. Gradually add the milk, mixing steadily to make a smooth thick sauce. Add salt, lots of fresh pepper, and cook over a low flame for about 15 minutes, stirring often to prevent a crust forming.

3. While the bechamel is cooking, cook fettuccine in a large pan of boiling salted water until barely *al dente* (see cooking instructions, Chapter 3). If using fresh fettuccine, boil only for a few minutes.

4. Add the cheese and remaining butter to the bechamel. Remove from flame, and mix in the egg yolks, one at a time. Taste for seasoning, and add nutmeg.

5. Preheat the oven to 400 degrees. Drain the pasta, and add to the cheese/bechamel sauce. Mix well, and gently fold in the beaten egg whites, gently folding over until the whites and fettuccine are well blended. Bake for 20 minutes, until the top is golden.

TAGLIOLINI AL FORNO

(Baked Wispy Pasta)

In this dish, all the cooking is done in the oven, the light angel-hair pasta simmering slowly in broth after first crisping. The resulting rich blend goes a long way.

INGREDIENTS:

1 lb. wispy little short pastas
  (tagliolini)
2 tablespoons breadcrumbs
1/3 cup butter
1/2 cup slightly sharp, well melting
  cheese, such as Cheddar
Salt
1/2 teaspoon cinnamon
3 cups vegetable broth

1. Preheat oven to 400 degrees.

2. Butter a good sized baking dish, and sprinkle the breadcrumbs over the bottom.

3. Divide the pasta, butter and cheese into thirds. Place a third of the pasta at the bottom of the baking dish, and dot the entire layer with a third of the butter, cut into small bits. Sprinkle over a third of the cheese. Repeat the layers twice, ending with a layer of remaining butter and cheese. Sprinkle the cinnamon across the top.

4. Place the dish in the preheated oven, and bake for about 7 minutes, until the top layer of noodles is golden and crisp. Have the vegetable broth ready to pour over the noodles. (If making fresh broth, you can add the broth vegetables as well to the pasta.)

5. When the top layer of pasta is golden, pour over the hot broth to cover, making sure that all the noodles are immersed. Continue to bake until almost all of the broth is absorbed, approximately 10 more minutes. Remove from oven and serve.

BAKED ORZO WITH A CHEESE/LEMON DILL SAUCE

Orzo are rice-shaped little pastas that have a smooth, rather slippery feel going down. This oven-baked pasticcio makes a nice first course, something like a risotto.

INGREDIENTS:
1 lb. orzo pasta (or other rice-sized pasta)
1 tablespoon freshly grated lemon rind (zest only)
1 small onion, finely chopped
1 celery stalk, finely chopped
2 tablespoons butter
2 tablespoons olive oil
3 tablespoons flour
2 cups vegetable broth
1 small bunch fresh dill, chopped
3/4 cup grated Parmesan

1. Preheat the oven to 375 degrees. Butter a large shallow baking dish and sprinkle with $1/2$ of the grated lemon rind.

2. In a heavy saucepan, cook the onion and celery in the butter and olive oil, stirring, until the celery is soft. Add the flour, mix and add the broth, whisking all the time. Bring to a boil, add the remaining lemon rind, salt and pepper to taste, and cook for about 3 minutes, until the sauce is smooth and thick.

3. Boil the orzo in a large pot of salted water until just *al dente* (see cooking instructions, Chapter 3). Drain, transfer to a large mixing bowl, add the sauce and mix well. Add the dill and grated cheese and mix again.

4. Transfer to the baking dish, and bake for 30 minutes, until the orzo is bubbling and slightly crusty. Allow to rest a few minutes before serving.

PASTICCIO DI RIGATONI CON CAVOLFIORE

(Rigatoni Pasticcio with Cauliflower)

In this dish, similar to the preceding recipe, pine nuts and raisins combine with lots of onions, cauliflower and a stronger taste of anchovies, to make an interesting, unusual pasta.

INGREDIENTS:

1 lb. rigatoni or penne
1 head cauliflower, broken into flowerets
6 medium onions, coarsely chopped
1/2 cup olive oil
1/4 cup pine nuts
2 cans anchovies, drained and chopped
1/4 cup small sultana raisins
1 small can tomato concentrate
1 good pinch saffron
1 tablespoon dried oregano
Salt and freshly ground pepper

1. Preheat oven to 350 degrees.

2. Fill a deep saucepan with enough water to later cook the pasta, add salt and bring to a boil. Add the cauliflower for about 5 minutes, or until it is almost cooked.

3. Drain the cauliflower, reserving the water, and set aside. Boil the water again, and cook the pasta until it is barely *al dente*. Drain, saving 1 cup of the water in which the cauliflower and pasta were cooked.

4. In a deep heavy pan, saute the chopped onions in the olive oil over a low flame until they are transparent. Add the pine nuts and saute for another minute. Add the chopped anchovies and the raisins. Dilute the tomato concentrate with 1/2 cup warm water and add, together with the saffron. Rub in the oregano, and add salt and freshly ground pepper to taste.

5. Combine the onion mixture with the cauliflower flowers and mix well. Add the drained noodles, mix again and pour the entire mixture into a casserole. Pour over the cup of drained pasta water, cover and bake for twenty minutes. Remove cover and bake for another five minutes.

PASTICCIO DI FETTUCCINE CON CAVOLO E PATATE

(Fettuccine Pasticcio with Cabbage and Potatoes)

A rustic dish that blends banal cabbage and potatoes with freshly made fettuccine. It's a nutritious, attractive and innovative family supper. This recipe serves six to eight.

INGREDIENTS:

1 lb. fresh wide fettuccine noodles
1 lb. potatoes, peeled and thinly sliced
1 large white cabbage, shredded
2 large onions, halved and thinly sliced
1 clove garlic, pressed
2 sprigs rosemary leaves, chopped
1/2 cup butter
1/2 cup grated Parmesan cheese
1 lb. mozzarella, thinly sliced
Salt and freshly ground pepper

1. Fill a pan large enough to hold potatoes, cabbage and pasta with salted water, and bring to the boil. Add the sliced potatoes and cook for 5 minutes. Add the shredded cabbage and cook for a few more minutes, until the potatoes are almost cooked but still hold their shape.

2. Add the fettuccine to the pot and continue to cook until the pasta is barely *al dente*, about 5 more minutes. Drain.

3. Put the onion slices, garlic, rosemary and butter into a saute pan, and cook slowly over a low flame until the onions are soft and transparent. Add the grated cheese and remove from heat. Mix together until the cheese is well melted into the onion sauce.

4. Preheat the oven to very hot (450 F.). Butter a large baking dish, and arrange all of the ingredients, including the sliced mozzarella, within reach. To assemble the pasticcio, spread a third of the potato/cabbage/fettuccine mixture at the bottom of the baking dish, cover with a third of the sliced mozzarella. Spread a third of the onion/cheese mixture on top, and sprinkle liberally with salt and freshly ground pepper.

5. Repeat twice more, ending up with a layer of the onion/cheese sauce. Put the casserole into the preheated oven for five minutes, or until the top is bubbling and brown. Allow to rest for another five minutes before serving.

PASTICCIO DI MACCHERONCINI CON CARNE

(Pasticcio of Macaroni and Chopped Beef)

A party dish or a family supper. It's best served in the simplest of baking dishes and brought crisp and steaming to the table. This version serves eight.

INGREDIENTS:
1 lb. small maccheroncini (the smallest tubed pastas)
1 medium onion, finely chopped
3 cloves garlic, finely chopped
¹/4 cup olive oil
1 small, or ¹/2 large, celery root, rinsed and finely chopped
1 lb. chopped lean beef
5 oz. fresh mushrooms, wiped clean and sliced with their stems
1 teaspoon beef soup powder
¹/2 cup boiling water
1 small can tomato concentrate
1 large can of crushed plum tomatoes
1 tablespoon olive oil
1 tablespoon oregano
Leaves of 5 sprigs basil, finely chopped
Leaves of 10 sprigs parsley, finely chopped
Salt and freshly ground pepper
A handful of fresh breadcrumbs

1. Put the chopped onion, garlic and olive oil in a heavy skillet and saute over a medium heat until the onion is transparent, about 3 minutes. Add the chopped celery root, and the chopped beef, and toss with two forks as the meat cooks and loses its red color.

2. Add the mushrooms, and mix well into the beef.

3. Dissolve the powdered soup in the boiling water, mix the resulting soup with the tomato concentrate and pour into the skillet. Add the tomatoes, of salt and some grindings of pepper. Mix well, cover and simmer for one hour. If mixture begins to dry, add a little beef stock.

4. Preheat the oven to medium (350⁰ F.). Cook the pasta in a large pan of boiling salted water until just *al dente* (see cooking instructions, Chapter 3). Drain and put in a wide, fairly shallow baking dish. Pour a tablespoon of olive oil over and mix well.

5. Add the oregano, parsley and basil to the meat sauce, taste for salt, and pour the entire mixture over the cooked pasta. Gently mix the sauce into the pasta, and sprinkle with a layer of breadcrumbs. Moisten the breadcrumbs with a dripping of olive oil, and bake for 30 minutes, until the entire dish is bubbling.

6. To make the mushroom/tomato sauce, soak dried mushrooms in hot water for 30 minutes, drain and reseve. Heat the oil, lightly fry the pressed garlic, then add mushrooms and saute. Add the drained porcini mushrooms to the pan, along with the chopped tomatoes and parsley leaves, and season with salt and pepper.

7. To assemble the *timballo*, fill the pie crust in layers, first a layer of gnocchi, then the sauce, the bechamel and a sprinkling of cheese. Repeat until all ingredients are used, and finish with the remaining cheese. Place in a hot oven for 10 minutes, remove sides of pan, gently slide onto a heat-proof serving dish and serve.

TIMBALLO DI SALMONE

(Timbale of Tagliatelle and Smoked Salmon)

Another party pasta, rich and filling. The greens are layered on the bottom of the pastry case, and covered with a lush smoked salmon tagliatelle filling. Then, the timballo is baked until it's crisp and golden on top; each slice is a layered contrast of greens and salmon-pink tagliatelle.

INGREDIENTS:
1 lb. fresh tagliatelle

Filling:
3/4 lb. Swiss chard or spinach
6 tablespoons olive oil
1/2 lb. small zucchini, sliced thinly
4 spring onions, sliced thinly
1/2 lb. smoked salmon, chopped into small pieces
1/4 cup dry vermouth
1 cup fresh cream

Crust:
1 1/4 cups flour
3/4 cup butter
Salt
Iced water

Mushroom bechamel:
2 tablespoons butter
5 oz. mushrooms, thinly sliced
2 tablespoons flour
1 1/2 cups milk
Salt and freshly ground pepper

1. Work the flour together with salt and butter until mixture resembles breadcrumbs, and add just enough ice water to make a dough. Work into a ball, wrap in wax paper and refrigerate while you make the sauce.

2. Cook the chard or spinach in boiling salted water. When cool, squeeze out all excess water and chop.

3. In a small pan, heat 3 tablespoons of the olive oil, add zucchini and half of the spring onions, and saute. Add chopped spinach, mix, and add salt. Remove from heat.

4. In another pan saute the remaining spring onion remaining olive oil, add the smoked salmon, cook 1 minute, then add the vermouth and allow to bubble out. Add the cream and season with salt.

5. To make the bechamel, melt 2 tablespoons butter and fry the sliced mushrooms for about two minutes, just until they begin to release water. Sprinkle over 2 tablespoons of flour, and add the milk. Stir constantly until the sauce is thick and smooth. Add the salmon/green onion cream sauce, and mix well, set aside.

6. Roll out the dough for the crust. Butter and flour a 9-inch spring form and line with rolled out dough. Leave an overhang of about 1/2 inch. Spread the spinach and zucchini mixture across the bottom. Cook the tagliatelle for about 3 minutes, drain and mix in the salmon/bechamel sauce. Spread over spinach mixture.

7. Preheat oven to high (400⁰ F). Cut off excess pastry around edges of baking pan, cover with tin foil and bake in preheated oven for about 12 minutes. Remove foil and bake for 12 more minutes, until the top is golden Remove sides of pan, gently slide the *timballo* onto a serving tray and serve hot.

TORTA DI PASTA

Without a crust, but made in a similar manner, this is an unusual and beautiful buffet dish, accompanied by a light tomato sauce on the side. This recipe serves at least 20 as part of a buffet, and probably more.

INGREDIENTS:
2 lbs. spaghetti
2 tablespoons butter
1/4 cup olive oil
4 medium onions, coarsely chopped
7 eggs
2 cups fresh cream
2 oz. smoked provolone cheese, grated
1/3 cup grated Parmesan
10 1/2 oz. mozzarella, grated
1 large bunch parsley leaves, chopped
Salt and lots of freshly ground pepper

Sauce:
1/2 cup olive oil
2 cloves garlic, pressed
1 cup ready made tomato sauce (see index)
1 bunch basil leaves, chopped

1. Preheat the oven to medium (350⁰ F). Butter a 9-inch spring form pan. Cook the pasta in a large pot of boiling water until just *al dente*. Drain well, splash over some cold water and set aside.

2. In a heavy skillet, heat together butter and olive oil until butter melts, add the chopped onions and saute until the onions are transparent. Turn off the flame.

3. In a large bowl , whisk together the eggs and cream, add the grated cheeses, the chopped parsley leaves, salt and freshly ground pepper to taste and the onion mixture.

4. Add the spaghetti and mix well. Pour the mixture into the buttered baking pan, place the pan on a baking sheet and bake for about 1 hour and 15 minutes, or until the top is firm to the touch at the center.

5. While the *torta* is baking, make the tomato sauce. Heat the oil and garlic together, add the tomato sauce (either bottled or your own) and cook over a lively flame for about five minutes. Add salt and pepper, and the chopped basil.

6. Remove sides of baking pan, and serve the *torta* warm, sliced into wedges, accompanied by the sauce.

CONCHIGLINI WITH A DILL VINAIGRETTE

A simple salad of nothing more than little pasta shells immersed in a soothing dressing flecked with dill. It's nice as a summer starter, or as part of an outdoor buffet when other salads tend to wilt. Be sure to give it an extra tossing just before serving.

INGREDIENTS:

1 lb. little pasta shells
Juice of one lemon
1 cup sour cream
2 teaspoons Dijon mustard
1 garlic clove, crushed
1 bunch dill, finely chopped
Salt and freshly ground pepper
2 tablespoons light olive oil

1. Mix together the lemon, the sour cream and mustard. Crush in the garlic clove, mix in the chopped dill. Add a teaspoon of salt and lots of freshly ground pepper. Store in refrigerator to allow flavors to blend.

2. Cook the shells in a large amount of boiling salted water until just *al dente* (see cooking instructions, Chapter 3). Drain well, and splash with cold water. Transfer to a work bowl, and mix well with the olive oil. Allow to cool completely, mixing every now and again to keep from sticking.

3. Mix in the dressing, turning round and round to make sure all the shells are coated. Mix again just before serving.

INSALATA DI FARFALLE AGLI AROMI

(Farfalle Salad with Herbs)

INGREDIENTS:

1 scant lb. farfalle, or other short pasta
1/2 lb. mushrooms
1/2 cup olive oil
1 tablespoon paprika
2 tablespoons white wine vinegar
Juice of 1 lemon
Salt and freshly ground pepper
1 small bunch of basil leaves, chopped
1 small bunch of parsley leaves, chopped
Leaves of 3 sprigs of fresh marjoram, or oregano, chopped
1 full sprig of fresh tarragon leaves, chopped
5 tablespoons mayonnaise
1 clove garlic, pressed
Soy sauce (optional)
1 stalk American celery, thinly sliced
3 spring onions, thinly sliced with as much green as is fresh

1. Wipe mushrooms, peel if necessary and slice thinly. Place the sliced mushrooms in a large bowl. Mix the olive oil, paprika, vinegar, lemon juice and salt. Beat together for a moment, and pour over the mushrooms.

2. Add the chopped herbs to the mushrooms. Mix well, and allow to marinate for at least half an hour.

3. Mix the mayonnaise with the garlic, the soy sauce, the sliced celery and spring onions.

4. Cook the pasta in a large amount of boiling salted water until just *al dente* (see cooking instructions, Chapter 3). Drain and splash with cold water, then drain again. Add mayonnaise immediately, mix well, pour over the marinated mushrooms and herbs and mix well again. Taste and season with salt and freshly ground pepper before serving.

INSALATA DI FUSILLI CON FUNGHI E ARANCIA

(Penne Salad with Mushrooms and Orange)

This is a favorite buffet dish. Lots of color and the taste of fresh citrus sharpened only slightly by the anchovies. I suggest roasting the peppers, but if time is a factor, it's not entirely necessary. Any short pasta will do here.

INGREDIENTS:
1 lb. fusilli, or other short pasta
2 red peppers, or one red, one yellow
1/2 lb. fresh mushrooms
4 oz. pitted black olives, coarsely chopped
1 can anchovy fillets, drained and chopped
2/3 cup fresh orange juice
1/4 cup olive oil
3 garlic cloves, crushed
Salt and freshly ground pepper
Small bunch mint or basil leaves, finely chopped

1. Roast peppers over a flame until black. Skin, remove seeds and inner ribs, and slice into thin strips.

2. Wipe mushrooms, peel if necessary, and slice thinly.

3. Mix the peppers, sliced mushrooms, chopped olives, chopped anchovy fillets, and orange juice, and chill.

4. Heat olive oil and garlic over a medium flame just until the oil around garlic begins to bubble. Remove from flame and allow to cool.

5. Cook the pasta in a large amount of boiling salted water until just *al dente* (see cooking instructions, Chapter 3). Drain and give a quick cold rinse. Mix together with the olive oil, making sure the pasta is completely coated. Allow to cool, mixing often to ensure that the pasta does not stick.

6. When the pasta is cool, and an hour or so before serving, mix well with the orange juice/vegetable marinade. Taste for seasoning, add of salt and lots of freshly ground pepper. Add the chopped mint or basil. Mix well over and over, and again before you serve.

CURRIED PASTA SALAD

A salad with lots of varied components and a taste of curry It can easily serve four or five as a main supper dish. If you are missing an ingredient, either eliminate it entirely or substitute another. The arugula is wonderful here, but any other bitter salad can serve.

INGREDIENTS:

1 lb. eliche, or spiral pasta
1/2 cup plus 2 tablespoons olive oil
2 large eggs
3 medium carrots, coarsely grated
2 large red peppers, seeds and ribs removed, sliced into thin strips
6 thin spring onions, sliced (if thick, halve lengthwise)
10 small radishes
2 bunches arugula
2 tablespoons sesame seeds
2 tablespoons curry powder
1/2 cup fresh cream
Salt and freshly ground pepper

1. Cook the pasta in a large amount of boiling salted water until just *al dente* (see cooking instructions, Chapter 3). Drain through a colander and splash with cold water. Mix well with 2 tablespoons of the olive oil and set aside.

2. Beat the eggs, and add salt to taste. Heat another tablespoon of olive oil in a large frying pan and make a thin omelet of the eggs. Remove, and allow to cool. When cool, roll the omelet and slice thinly.

3. Place the grated carrots, the peppers, the sliced onion, radishes and arugula in a large serving bowl. Add the slices of omelet and pasta, sprinkle over the sesame seeds and mix well.

4. In a smaller bowl, dissolve the curry powder in the cream and mix in the remaining olive oil. Salt well and pour over the salad. Mix well and serve.

ORZO SALAD WITH ARTICHOKES

Orzo is the little oval pasta that resembles oversized rice. This cold dish of orzo combined with artichokes in a rich mayonnaise sauce should not stand too long before serving.

INGREDIENTS:

1 cup orzo (rice-shaped pasta)
3/4 cup olive oil
1/2 lb. artichoke hearts.
1/2 cup vegetable broth
1 large egg yolk
2 tablespoons white wine vinegar
1 teaspoon Dijon-type mustard
5 sprigs fresh basil, chopped
1/3 cup grated Parmesan cheese
2 tablespoons fresh lemon juice,
1 small bunch parsley, leaves, chopped
5 small spring onions, finely chopped

1. Cook the orzo in plenty of boiling salted water until just *al dente*. Drain, rinse with cold water and toss with 1/4 cup of the olive oil. Cut the artichoke hearts into small pieces and simmer in broth for about 7 minutes, until just tender. Drain and add to orzo.

2. To make mayonnaise, beat the egg yolk with the vinegar, mustard, a teaspoon of salt and lots of freshly ground pepper. Slowly add the remaining 1/2 cup oil. When mixture reaches mayonnaise consistency, whisk in the minced basil and mix with the orzo and artichokes. Add the Parmesan, the lemon juice (taste as you pour), parsley, spring onions, and salt and pepper to taste. Toss well and garnish with basil leaves. Serve at room temperature.

PENNE ROSA

(Rose-colored Penne Salad)

A cup of yoghurt plus a goodly addition of olives, capers and tomatoes makes an inviting luncheon salad. Make the dressing while the pasta cooks.

INGREDIENTS:

1 lb. penne, or any other short, tubular pasta
1/2 cup plus 2 tablespoons olive oil
5 fresh ripe tomatoes
1 cup plain yoghurt
1/4 cup grated Parmesan cheese
Small bunch basil leaves, coarsely chopped
3 or 4 sprigs of fresh oregano leaves, coarsely chopped
10 pitted black olives, coarsely chopped
10 pitted green olives, coarsely chopped
1 tablespoon capers, drained and coarsely chopped
2 garlic cloves, crushed
Salt and freshly ground pepper
Leaves of a few sprigs parsley, chopped

1. Cook the penne in a large pan of boiling salted water until just *al dente* (see cooking instructions, Chapter 3). Drain, splash with cold water, and drain again. Mix with 2 tablespoons olive oil, and cool thoroughly. Mix occasionally to ensure that the pasta does not stick.

2. Halve the tomatoes, squeeze to remove all seeds and juice, and slice to strips about the width of the cooked penne.

3. Make the dressing. Mix the yoghurt and grated cheese; add the chopped herbs, olives, capers, garlic and remaining olive oil. Fold in the sliced tomatoes. Taste for seasoning, add about a teaspoon of salt and lots of freshly ground pepper.

4. Mix the dressing completely with the penne, taste again for seasoning, sprinkle over the parsley and serve.

MEDITERRANEAN SALAD

Cube the vegetables to match the size of the pasta you use for this recipe. Recommended are the littlest shells; the bits of vegetables find their way into the crevices and make for lots of interesting tastes. The salad is best when mixed at the last minute.

INGREDIENTS:
³/4 lb. conchiglie (shells)
¹/2 cup plus 2 tablespoons olive oil
1 medium eggplant, peeled and diced into small cubes
frying oil (preferable light olive)
1 red pepper, seeded, ribs removed, diced into small cubes
1 yellow pepper, seeded, ribs removed, diced into small cubes
15 black olives, stoned and chopped
1 can anchovies, finely chopped
3 cloves garlic, crushed
3 tablespoons red wine vinegar
Salt and freshly ground pepper
Leaves of about 10 sprigs parsley, coarsely chopped
Leaves of about 5 sprigs basil, coarsely chopped

1. The pieces of vegetables should all be about the same size or smaller than the shells you are using. Salt the eggplant liberally, place in a colander to drain for at least half an hour. (On a dry day, place them on a paper outside and the sun will dry the bitter juices as they run.)

2. Squeeze the eggplant dry (if necessary) and fry until crisp. Drain on absorbent paper until the eggplant is completely free of grease and you are ready to mix the salad.

3. Combine the chopped peppers with the olives, the anchovies, crushed garlic, vinegar and ¹/2 cup olive oil. Add some freshly ground pepper, and set aside while the pasta is cooking.

4. Cook the pasta in a large amount of boiling salted water until just *al dente* (see cooking instructions, Chapter 3). Drain and splash some cold water over, drain again, and mix in a large bowl with the remaining two tablespoons olive oil. Allow to cool, mixing every now and again to keep from sticking.

5. Before serving, add the olive oil and vinegar dressing to the pasta and mix well. Add the cubed eggplant and chopped herbs and mix again. Taste for salt, and add some freshly ground pepper as well. Serve immediately, or as soon as possible.

FARFALLE SALAD WITH AVOCADO/LEMON CREAM

This is almost a guacamole salad dressing, with chopped tomato, spring onions and coriander perking up a rather pale look. It's a nice salad that goes alongside a tossed green salad very amenably.

INGREDIENTS:
³/₄ lb. farfalle, or dischi volente, or any other small flat pasta
¹/₂ cup plus 2 tablespoons olive oil
1 large avocado, very ripe
Juice and grated rind of 1 large lemon
2 garlic cloves, crushed
Salt and freshly ground pepper
1 tablespoon vinegar (if necessary)
3 tomatoes, skinned, seeded, drained and chopped well
4 spring onions, thinly sliced with as much of the green as is fresh
1 small bunch coriander, finely chopped (or parsley)

1. Cook the pasta in a large amount of boiling water until just barely *al dente* (see cooking instructions, Chapter 3). Drain, splash with cold water, drain again and toss immediately with 2 tablespoons olive oil until well coated. Allow to cool, stirring occasionally to ensure that the pasta does not stick.

2. Prepare the dressing. Scoop the flesh out of the avocado and place in a food processor, together with the lemon juice and rind, the crushed garlic, salt and freshly ground pepper. Turn on the machine, and begin to add the oil, slowly, forming a kind of mayonnaise. Remove to a bowl, taste for salt, and add some freshly ground pepper. The dressing should be somewhat tangy; if too mild, add a tablespoon of white wine vinegar.

3. Mix the cooled pasta with the dressing, taste again and add some more salt and pepper. Add the chopped tomatoes, spring onion and chopped coriander and mix again before serving. The salad should not be refrigerated; if you must do so, bring to room temperature before serving.

FIORI CON SALMONE AFFUMICATO

(Pasta Flowers with Smoked Salmon)

There's a wonderful fresh pasta available that is perfect for pasta salads. It resembles a kind of open lily flower. If not available, I suggest using the dried farfalle for this rather luxurious pasta salad.

INGREDIENTS:
3/4 lbs. fresh fiori pasta, or dried farfalle
5 oz. smoked salmon
1 cup sour cream
1/4 cup plus 2 tablespoons fresh olive oil
3 tablespoons fresh lemon juice
1 tablespoon Dijon mustard
1 tablespoon dry white wine
Freshly ground white pepper
1 small red onion, thinly sliced
1/4 cup freshly chopped chives
1 small bunch dill, well chopped
2 tablespoons capers, drained and coarsely chopped
Salt and more pepper to taste

1. Cut the salmon into thin strips, and reserve in the refrigerator.

2. To make the dressing, combine the sour cream, 1/4 cup of the olive oil, the lemon juice, mustard, wine and lots of freshly ground white pepper. Whisk together until amalgamated, and store in refrigerator.

3. Cook the pasta in a large amount of boiling salted water until just barely *al dente* (see cooking instructions, Chapter 3). Drain, toss well with the remaining 2 tablespoons olive oil, and transfer to a serving bowl. Mix occasionally to prevent sticking.

4. Add the onion, chives, dill and chopped capers to the pasta, and toss again. Allow to cool completely. Add the salmon and the dressing, and refrigerate until ready to serve.

TWO-SALMON PASTA SALAD

Two kinds of salmons - smoked and filleted - combine with peas to make a colorful cold supper dish. Use a whole milk yoghurt.

INGREDIENTS:
1 lb. short ribbed pasta (penne rigate, sedani, etc.)
5 oz. smoked salmon, thinly sliced and cut into thin strips
5 oz. fresh cooked salmon, flaked
1 stalk celery, thinly sliced
1 1/2 cups whole milk yoghurt
1 teaspoon mustard
1 small bunch dill, chopped
2 tablespoons olive oil
Salt to taste
Pinch hot pepper powder
1/2 cup small peas, barely cooked
1/2 large lemon

1. Mix the two salmons and sliced celery with the yoghurt, mustard, dill, olive oil, salt to taste and hot pepper (the taste should be slightly piquant). Add the peas and lemon juice, and mix gently again. Refrigerate until ready to mix into the pasta.

2. Cook the pasta in lots of boiling salted water until just *al dente*, splash under cold water and drain again. Add the salmon sauce. Mix well, taste for seasoning, add salt and freshly ground white pepper, and serve.

FUSILLI WITH FETA AND GARLIC DRESSING

Fusilli with a Greek Salad dressing. The pasta not only takes the salad further, but soothes the sharpness as well.

INGREDIENTS:
1 lb. fusilli, or any other short pasta
¹/2 cup plus 2 tablespoons olive oil
3 medium tomatoes, halved, squeezed free of inner juice and seeds, and sliced thinly.
5 spring onions, sliced into ¹/4 inch pieces, with as much of their green as is fresh.
3 ¹/2 oz. feta cheese, broken up into small bite-sized pieces
3-4 pickled pimentos, sliced into thin strips
1 small can anchovies, chopped (optional)
25-30 black olives in brine, pitted and halved
2 garlic cloves, pressed
Juice of 1 lemon (or more, according to taste)
5 sprigs oregano leaves, chopped (or 2 tablespoons dried, rubbed through the palms)
Small bunch basil leaves, chopped
Small bunch parsley leaves, chopped
Salt and freshly ground pepper

1. Cook the pasta in a large pan of boiling salted water until just *al dente* (see cooking instructions, Chapter 3). Drain, splash with cold water, drain again and mix with 2 tablespoons of the olive oil. Continue to mix occasionally to ensure that the pasta does not stick.

2. Halve the tomatoes, squeeze to remove inner juice and seeds, and slice thinly. Set aside. Slice spring onions into ¹/4 inch pieces, with as much of their green as is fresh.

3. Mix the tomatoes, spring onions, feta, pimentos, anchovy fillets, olives and tomatoes in a large bowl that will hold the pasta as well. Mix well.

4. In a small bowl, or jar, place all ingredients for the dressing: crushed garlic, lemon juice, herbs, salt, lots of freshly ground pepper, and the remaining olive oil. close tightly and shake well

5. Pour the pasta into the vegetable bowl, toss well together. Pour over the dressing and mix again. Taste for seasoning, add some more freshly ground pepper on top and serve.

CHICKEN/FUSILLI SALAD WITH VINAIGRETTE DRESSING

A splendid summer buffet: chicken salad with a light oil and vinegar dressing.

INGREDIENTS:

1 lb. fusilli or any other short pasta
1/2 cup plus 2 tablespoons olive oil
About 1 lb. cooked chicken or turkey, diced
2 tablespoons capers
2 small firm pickles, chopped

1 brined red pepper, coarsely chopped
Small bunch parsley leaves
2 tablespoons wine vinegar
1 garlic clove, pressed
Salt and freshly ground pepper

1. Cook the pasta in a large amount of boiling salted water until just *al dente* (see cooking instructions, Chapter 3). Drain, splash with cold water, and drain again. Mix thoroughly with 2 tablespoons of the olive oil, making sure all the pasta is coated. Cool, mixing every now and again to ensure that the pasta does not stick.

2. Combine the chicken, capers, pickles, red pepper and chopped parsley in another bowl. In a small bowl, crush the garlic into the remaining olive oil, and mix well. Pour in the vinegar, mix again and pour the dressing into the chicken mixture.

3. Pour the chicken dressing over the pasta, add salt and lots of freshly ground pepper, and mix well. Taste for seasoning. If you prefer the salad sharper, add another tablespoon of vinegar. Keep tossing as you serve to make sure each portion is well covered with vinaigrette.

MAYONNAISE-DRESSED CHICKEN PASTA SALAD

A more traditional mayonnaise chicken salad, Don't allow it to stand around too long on a hot summer day.

INGREDIENTS:

1/2 lb. maccheroncini, or any other short, tubular pasta
4 tablespoons olive oil
3 spring onions
About 1 lb. cold cooked chicken or turkey
1 tablespoon Dijon mustard
1/2 cup mayonnaise

Juice of 1 lemon
2 firm pickles, sliced into matchstick lengths
1 tablespoon capers, coarsely chopped
Salt and freshly ground pepper to taste

1. Cook the pasta in a large amount of boiling salted water until just *al dente*. Drain, splash with cold water, and drain again. Mix well with 2 tablespoons of the olive oil.

2. Slice spring onions into 1/2 inch lengths, using as much of the green as is edible. If onions are thick, halve lengthwise first. Thinly slice chicken, and cut into thin matchsticks about the length of the pasta.

3. In a large bowl, whisk together the mustard, mayonnaise, lemon juice and remaining 2 tablespoons olive oil into a creamy sauce. Add the pickles, spring onions, capers and salt with lots of freshly ground pepper. Stir in the chicken, and store in the refrigerator until ready to serve.

4. Mix the pasta well with the chicken dressing, taste for seasoning and add salt. If the salad seems too dry, add some olive oil to moisten, mix well and serve immediately.

GARDEN SALAD OVER A HOT PASTA

A very popular summer pasta in Italy, this pasta cannot truly be termed a salad. It's a last minute dish that combines fresh uncooked summer vegetables, a touch of lemon juice, and a steaming pasta.

INGREDIENTS:

1 lb. spaghettini or any other long, fine pasta
1 lb. tomatoes
1 green pepper, seeded, ribs removed, thinly sliced
1 red pepper, seeded, ribs removed, thinly sliced
2 small zucchini, sliced into matchsticks

Small bunch fresh basil leaves, coarsely chopped
1/2 cup plus 2 tablespoons olive oil
Juice of 1-2 lemons
Salt and freshly ground pepper

1. Skin tomatoes, seed, quarter and slice thinly. Drain tomatoes well for half an hour after they have been sliced.

2. While the tomatoes are draining, combine the other salad ingredients: the sliced peppers, zucchini, basil, 1/2 cup olive oil and lemon juice. Season with salt and lots of freshly ground pepper. Add the tomatoes and continue to marinate while the pasta cooks.

3. Cook the pasta in a large amount of boiling salted water until just *al dente* (see cooking instructions, Chapter 3). Drain, and pour into a heated serving dish. Pour over the remaining 2 tablespoons olive oil, and mix well.

4. Mix half the salad into the pasta and toss well. As soon as the first half of the salad is mixed in, pour over the remaining salad and serve immediately.

FARFALLE RICCHE

(Farfalle with Tongue)

A vinaigrette salad of shaped pasta with tongue. Smoked tongue gives a special flavor, but a plain boiled one will do as well.

INGREDIENTS:

1 scant lb. farfalle or other flat pasta
1/2 cup plus 2 tablespoons olive oil
5 ripe tomatoes
3 spring onions
10 1/2 oz. smoked tongue, cubed into 1/4 inch cubes

1 medium cucumber, peeled and thinly sliced
1/2 teaspoon paprika
1 teaspoon mustard
2 teaspoons wine vinegar
Salt and freshly ground pepper,
1 bunch parsley leaves, chopped

1. Cook the pasta in a large pan of boiling salted water until just barely *al dente*. Run quickly under some cold water, drain and place in a large bowl. Mix with 2 tablespoons of the olive oil, making sure all of the pasta is well covered.

2. Skin tomatoes, halve, squeeze free of juice and seeds, and slice thinly. Slice spring onions into 1/4 inch pieces with as much green as is fresh.

3. Add tomatoes, spring onions, tongue, and sliced cucumber to cooked pasta and mix well.

4. In a serving bowl that will hold the salad, mix the paprika, the mustard, vinegar, remaining olive oil, salt and pepper. Add the pasta and vegetables, and mix well together. Place in the refrigerator for about 15 minutes to cool, sprinkle over some chopped parsley leaves and serve.

PASTA SALAD WITH FILLET OF SOLE

The use of fresh sole makes a difference here. If using frozen, I would suggest halibut, which holds its shape better and seems to have a fuller flavor than the frozen sole.

INGREDIENTS:
3/4 lb. small conchiglie (shells)

COURT BOUILLON:
1 small carrot, sliced
1 small onion, sliced
1 stalk celery, sliced
2 sprigs parsley
1 bay leaf
Juice of 1 large lemon
Salt and freshly ground pepper

2 large fillets of fresh sole or frozen halibut
2 large peppers, one red, one yellow
2 large firm tomatoes, skinned, seeded, drained and sliced into thin strips
5 oz. pitted black olives, halved or quartered
1 small bunch parsley leaves, chopped
1 clove garlic, pressed
1/3 cup olive oil

1. Make a court bouillon for the fish. Place the carrot, onion, celery, parsley, bay leaf' lemon juice, salt and pepper in a deep saute pan. Add about 2 cups of water and simmer for half an hour. Add the sole fillets and cook gently until just done. Allow to cool in the bouillon, remove and break into small strips. Reserve bouillon.

2. Roast the peppers over an open flame. Skin, remove seeds and inner ribs and cut into thin strips.

3. Put peppers and tomatoes into a large serving bowl, and add the olives, chopped parsley, pressed garlic and olive oil. Add the fish slices and about 2 tablespoons of the cooking bouillon. (Reserve the remainder for possible use when salad is mixed.)

4. Cook the pasta in a large amount of boiling salted water until just *al dente*. Drain, run under cold water, drain again, and add immediately to the fish mixture. Mix gently but thoroughly.

5. Taste and add salt and freshly ground pepper. If pasta seems too dry, add some of the fish bouillon. Serve immediately.

TUNA AND MACCHERONCINI SALAD

This recipe is but a suggestion of the vegetables that can be combined with a can of tuna fish and pasta, to make a lovely and nutritious summer salad. Use whatever vegetables you have on hand; almost anything works.

INGREDIENTS:

1/2 lb. maccheroncini, or any other short pasta
Juice of 1 lemon
1/4 cup white wine
1 tablespoon Dijon mustard
1 cup sour cream
Small bunch dill, chopped
1 teaspoon Worcestershire sauce (optional)
Pinch of sugar
2 tablespoons olive oil
2 light green peppers, seeded, ribs removed, coarsely chopped
1 red pepper, seeded, ribs removed, coarsely chopped
2 fresh tomatoes, drained, seeded and coarsely chopped
2 small cucumbers, diced
1 tablespoon capers, coarsely chopped
1 large can white-meat tuna (6 oz.)
Salt and freshly ground pepper

1. Prepare the dressing: Combine the lemon juice, wine and mustard in a bowl, and slowly whisk in the sour cream. Stir in the chopped dill, the Worcestershire sauce and a pinch of sugar. Mix well and refrigerate.

2. Cook the pasta in a large pan of boiling salted water until just *al dente* (see cooking instructions, Chapter 3). Drain, splash some cold water over, and drain again. Toss with 2 tablespoons of olive oil until all the pasta is coated. Cool, stirring occasionally to keep the pasta from sticking.

3. Combine the peppers, tomatoes, cucumbers and capers in a large bowl and toss together. Break the tuna into small pieces and add, gently mixing in with the vegetables.

4. Just before serving, add the cooled pasta to the vegetables and tuna, pour over the chilled dressing and mix well. Taste for salt and add lots of freshly ground pepper as well. Serve immediately.

RECIPES WITH ITALIAN NAMES